Electronic Legal Research:
An Integrated Approach

The West Legal Studies Series

Your options keep growing with West Legal Studies

Each year our list continues to offer you more options for every area of the law to meet your course or on-the-job reference requirements. We now have over 140 titles from which to choose in the following areas:

Administrative Law	Family Law
Alternative Dispute Resolution	Federal Taxation
Bankruptcy	Intellectual Property
Business Organizations/Corporations	Introduction to Law
Civil Litigation and Procedure	Introduction to Paralegalism
CLA Exam Preparation	Law Office Management
Client Accounting	Law Office Procedures
Computer in the Law Office	Legal Research, Writing, and Analysis
Constitutional Law	Legal Terminology
Contract Law	Paralegal Employment
Criminal Law and Procedure	Real Estate Law
Document Preparation	Reference Materials
Environmental Law	Torts and Personal Injury Law
Ethics	Will, Trusts, and Estate Administration

You will find unparalleled, practical support

Each book is augmented by instructor and student supplements to ensure the best learning experience possible. We also offer custom publishing and other benefits such as West's Student Achievement Award. In addition, our sales representatives are ready to provide you with dependable service.

We want to hear from you

Our best contributions for improving the quality of our books and instructional materials is feedback from the people who use them. If you have a question, concern, or observation about any of our materials, or you have a product proposal or manuscript, we want to hear from you. Please contact your local representative or write us at the following address:

West Legal Studies, 3 Columbia Circle, P.O. Box 15015, Albany, NY 12212-5015

For additional information point your browser at
www.westlegalstudies.com

WEST
THOMSON LEARNING

Electronic Legal Research:
An Integrated Approach

Stephanie Delaney, JD
Highline Community College

WEST

THOMSON LEARNING ™

Australia   Canada   Mexico   Singapore   Spain   United Kingdom   United States

WEST

THOMSON LEARNING

WEST LEGAL STUDIES

Electronic Legal Research: An Integrated Approach

by Stephanie Delaney

Business Unit Director:
Susan L. Simpfenderfer

Executive Editor:
Marlene McHugh Pratt

Senior Acquisitions Editor:
Joan M. Gill

Developmental Editor:
Rhonda Dearborn

Editorial Assistant:
Lisa Flatley

Executive Production Manager:
Wendy A. Troeger

Production Manager:
Carolyn Miller

Production Coordinator:
Matthew J. Williams

Executive Marketing Manager:
Donna J. Lewis

Channel Manager:
Nigar Hale

Cover Design:
Kristina Almquist Design

For permission to use material from this text or product, contact us by
Tel (800) 730-2214
Fax (800) 730-2215
www.thomsonrights.com

Library of Congress Cataloging-in-Publication Data
Delaney, Stephanie.
    Electronic legal research : an integrated
    approach/Stephanie Delaney. p. cm.
    "West Legal Studies Series."
    Includes index.
    ISBN: 0-7668-3006-3
    1. Legal research–United States–Data processing.
    2. Information storage and retrieval
    systems–Law–United States. I. Title.
KF242.A1 D45 2001
340'.0285–dc21

2001035981

NOTICE TO THE READER

Publisher does not warrant or guarantee any of the products described herein or perform any independent analysis in connection with any of the product information contained herein. Publisher does not assume, and expressly disclaims, any obligation to obtain and include information other than that provided to it by the manufacturer.

The reader is notified that this text is an educational tool, not a practice book. Since the law is in constant change, no rule or statement of law in this book should be relied upon for any service to any client. The reader should always refer to standard legal sources for the current rule or law. If legal advice or other expert assistance is required, the services of the appropriate professional should be sought.

The Publisher makes no representation or warranties of any kind, including but not limited to, the warranties of fitness for particular purpose or merchantability, nor are any such representations implied with respect to the material set forth herein, and the publisher takes no responsibility with respect to such material. The publisher shall not be liable for any special, consequential, or exemplary damages resulting, in whole or part, from the readers' use of, or reliance upon, this material.

Table of Contents

Part II - What to Search For

Dedication

This book is dedicated to my parents
Otis and Winona Delaney
who have supported me in everything.

Preface

"Give a person a fish and they eat for a day,

Teach a person to fish and they eat for a lifetime."

Ancient Chinese Proverb

As the power and convenience of electronic legal research continues to penetrate the legal world, schools scramble to train students how to use the newest research tools. The few textbooks that touch on this subject seem to spoon-feed students information: "Here's how to log on to Westlaw." "This is a good Internet site for researching statutes." In essence, those texts give students fish. This text is different. For law and paralegal students, lawyers, paralegals, legal secretaries, or anyone wanting to learn more about legal research, *Electronic Legal Research: An Integrated Approach* explains the how and the why of legal research. It fully explains rationale of putting together a query and guides readers through the steps to determine their own best site for researching statutes. *Electronic Legal Research: An Integrated Approach* teaches readers to fish the changing seas of electronic legal research. They will be competent to fish for a lifetime.

Electronic Legal Research: An Integrated Approach explores the topic of database searching with substance and depth in order to facilitate long-term learning. However, this text does not attempt to cover every kind of computer-based legal research. New products are introduced every day, and the market leaders constantly change. Rather than try to discuss each database separately, this text takes the approach that one set of skills—Boolean searching—will enable the student researcher to do research in nearly any electronic database. This text teaches those skills, specifically training students to research paid legal databases and the Internet using methods that they can apply to any other electronic database.

Electronic Legal Research: An Integrated Approach is based on the concept of critical thinking, the process of carefully considering information to determine its veracity and usefulness. In the context of research, critical thinking enables the student to make intelligent decisions about how to find information through effective resource selection and query construction. Rather than a traditional how-to book, *Electronic Legal Research: An Integrated Approach* truly facilitates student learning by presenting comprehensive information and challenging exercises that focus on critical thinking skills and practical skill implementation.

The comprehensive, critical thinking approach taken in *Electronic Legal Research: An Integrated Approach* makes it a useful research guide for both students and working professionals, for both paralegals and attorneys. Current manuals on computer-assisted legal research are segmented, covering only the Internet or just Westlaw or Lexis. *Electronic Legal Research: An Integrated Approach* pulls the resources together and demonstrates how the same set of skills can apply to most research. In addition, currently available research manuals give information without explaining how that information was arrived at or why the information is valid. *Electronic Legal Research: An Integrated Approach* presents students with the logic behind the information. So, when the information becomes outdated (as quickly happens in the electronic world), readers have the skills to find their own way. That makes *Electronic Legal Research: An Integrated Approach* different, and this difference enables readers to maximize their research potential.

Why I Wrote This Text

Learning effective research skills can be very difficult. Traditionally, students who excelled in the area often did so through luck or sheer determination. *Electronic Legal Research: An Integrated Approach* aims to level the playing field by providing clear, understandable steps to creating effective searches in nearly any database. It teaches the process of electronic legal research in a user-friendly, accessible tone that invites students to achieve research excellence.

In this information age, legal professionals rely more and more on database information retrieval—not only in legal research, but also in managing litigation documents, client files, and calendaring systems. Skills used for information retrieval are the same skills used for legal research, and this text helps students make that connection. When students do not realize this, each new database can seem intimidating. I wrote this book primarily to share this valuable information and to remove fear and intimidation from legal research.

Organization of the Text

Electronic Legal Research: An Integrated Approach uses a completely unique approach to teaching research online. Rather than dedicating a chapter to Lexis and Westlaw and another to the Internet, the text takes an integrated approach, showing that one research skill can provide success in most research arenas.

Electronic Legal Research: An Integrated Approach focuses on research strategies and query formation based on Boolean search operators.

Electronic Legal Research: An Integrated Approach shows that Boolean searching is the basis of all electronic research; if students can do an effective Boolean search, they can search for anything anywhere. Through integrated exercises, the student learns that Lexis, Westlaw, and the Internet are not all that different from each other and that the same set of skills leads them to successful results in each arena. Because of that, students develop the flexibility needed to adapt to the quickly changing seas of electronic research.

The text is divided into two parts. Part One (Chapters 1 through 4) explains How to Search. Chapters 1 and 2 explain the basics of searching computer databases using effective queries. These chapters also give students some general query-forming strategies. Chapters 3 and 4 explain how to apply the query strategies to a variety of databases, including Westlaw, Lexis, and the Internet.

Part Two (Chapters 5 through 8) focuses on Where to Search. It applies the strategies of Part One to specific types of legal research, including statutes, regulations, case law, and secondary sources. The idea is to integrate research strategies with the information sources. When this happens, the student can decide effectively where to look for the information she wants and knows exactly how to get it.

Within Chapters 5 through 8 students learn how to use paid legal databases and the Internet to create effective queries. Students learn to efficiently find the information they need using the information they have. Students will also learn how to compare the merits of each research resource when more than one is available, so that their research process can be effective and efficient.

Most texts that touch on electronic legal research include step-by-step how-to sections on Lexis and Westlaw. This text does not. These products change rapidly. Indeed, legal professionals everywhere are abandoning the traditional software-based Lexis and Westlaw in favor of using the Internet versions of these products. With such constant change in the legal research world, *Electronic Legal Research: An Integrated Approach* relies on the training materials that Westlaw, Lexis, and other paid legal databases provide to their subscribers. These materials do an excellent job of covering the basics of how to use their products. This text then provides a coherent, integrated approach to searching the databases using the Boolean search strategies.

Features of the Text

- **Encourages critical thinking.** *Electronic Legal Research: An Integrated Approach* applies the critical thinking model of learning. Rather than spoon-feeding the student with popular Web sites and simplistic Westlaw queries, it engages the student with the actual elements of query formation. The student is guided in *how* to learn, not simply told what to learn. This subtle yet significant shift in instruction enables the student to come to his or her own learning realizations. Students remember things better when they figure them out themselves.

- **Thought-provoking exercises.** To implement the critical thinking model, each learning section has thought-provoking exercises.
  - **Guided Exercises.** These in-depth exercises lead the student through the steps necessary to learn a new skill. Then additional exercises encourage the student to reflect on what he learned.
  - **Side notes.** Throughout the text, side notes alert students to common errors and other things to consider as they research.
- **Exercise worksheets.** Worksheets help the student work through the material in the chapter. They appeal to the visual learner. The worksheets provide an alternative presentation of the information in each chapter in a format that can be immediately applied to learning.
- **Web page.** An informative Web page complements and updates the text, helping students and teachers stay abreast of rapid changes in the legal research world. It also includes additional exercises for students who feel challenged by the materials.

How to Use This Text

Instructors can use the text in one of two ways. First, the text can be a companion to a current legal research text. Most legal research texts touch lightly on electronic legal research. By using this text with a regular legal research text, instructors can easily integrate electronic legal research into every component of learning. The short chapters and no-nonsense approach make this text an ideal tool for a holistic approach to research.

Electronic Legal Research: An Integrated Approach can also be used a stand-alone text for an advanced legal research class. (The text does not include enough basic research information for an introductory legal research class.) Experienced legal research students can achieve a new level of skill and comfort with their research abilities. Using the text in this manner also gives the student a chance to reinforce information learned in earlier legal research classes.

Whether used as a companion or stand-alone text, the features of *Electronic Legal Research: An Integrated Approach* facilitate comprehensive learning. Each chapter contains a Guided Exercise to help the student work through research problems logically, using information learned in the text. In later chapters, Guided Exercises also keep the foundation information, learned in Part One, fresh in students' minds. This facilitates comprehensive rather than compartmental learning.

Chapter Review Exercises give students opportunities to implement their learning. Exercise questions require students to incorporate information from earlier chapters, to facilitate an holistic approach to research. In keeping with the critical thinking approach of the text, each exercise question requires actual thought—the student cannot simply copy an answer from the text. This again enforces student learning and empowers students to truly learn valuable research skills.

Worksheets in each chapter give students a visual way to manage and incorporate information learned in the chapter. Many worksheets are useful for several different chapters, helping to reinforce the information learned in earlier chapters and enhancing the comprehensive approach to research.

To facilitate ease of use, exercises and worksheets are perforated for removal from the textbook. This feature is intended to encourage students to create their own useful reference notebook. The author has discovered that students appreciate the opportunity to use a binder and create a quick reference notebook to use while researching. Students can remove completed exercises, and worksheets, and put them in a binder, together with computer printouts, class handouts, and other information they gather on electronic legal research. This notebook of documents provides an easily updatable reference tool that students can use long after they leave the classroom. Both methods give the student an updateable resource that ensures that they will not forget their newly learned skills.

Supplemental Material

- **Instructor's Manual with Test Bank.** Written by the author of this text and available exclusively online, the Instructor's Manual contains chapter introductions, suggestions for emphasis, and teaching tips. It also includes answers to exercises, along with information on how to find answers, and ideas on crafting additional exercises. This manual should prove useful to instructors who are themselves learning to master electronic research. The Instructor's Manual can be found online at **www.westlegalstudies.com**. Please click Resources, then go to the Instructor's Lounge.

- **Computerized Test Bank.** The Test Bank in the Instructor's Manual is also available in computerized format on CD-ROM. Platforms supported include Windows™ 3.1 and 95, Windows NT, and Macintosh. Features include
  - multiple methods of question selection
  - multiple outputs, that is, print, ASCII and RTF
  - graphic support (black and white)
  - random questioning output
  - special character support

- **Web page.** Come visit us at **www.westlegalstudies.com**, where you will find materials and exercises to supplement this text. The Web page includes text updates and information to keep students current about the regularly changing world of electronic legal research. The Web page will also host the same worksheets found in the text, as well as useful links for students and instructors. This information is designed to help the student move from theory to practice.

  This is a restricted area that requires a username and password to gain access. You will find your username and password information below. You will need these to enter the restricted area, and you must enter the username and password exactly as they appear.

  The Online Resources Web site can be found at www.westlegalstudies.com. Please click Resources, then go to Online Resources.
  username: w4e5s6t7
  password: w8c9a2k9

- **Survival Manual for Paralegal Students.** Written by Bradene Moore and Kathleen Reed of the University of Toledo, the manual covers practical and basic information to help students make the most of their paralegal courses. Topics covered include choosing courses of study and note-taking skills. ISBN 0-314-22111-5.

- **Strategies and Tips for Paralegal Educators.** Written by Anita Tebbe of Johnson County Community College, this pamphlet provides teaching strategies specifically designed for paralegal educators. A copy is available to each adopter. Quantities for distribution to adjunct instructors are available for purchase at a minimal price. A coupon in the pamphlet provides ordering information. ISBN 0-314-04971-1.

- **Citation-at-a-Glance.** This handy reference card provides a quick, portable reference to the basic rules of citation for the most commonly cited legal sources, including judicial opinions, statutes, and secondary sources. *Citation-at-a-Glance* uses the rules set forth in *The Bluebook: A Uniform System of Citation*. Every student text includes a free copy of this valuable supplement.

- **WESTLAW®.** West's online computerized legal research system offers students hands-on experience with a system commonly used in law offices. Qualified adopters can receive ten free hours of WESTLAW. WESTLAW can be accessed with Macintosh and IBM PCs and compatibles. A modem is required.

- **Court TV videos.** West Legal Studies is pleased to offer the following videos from Court TV for a minimal fee:
  - *New York v. Ferguson—Murder on the 5:33: The Trial of Colin Ferguson.* ISBN 0-7668-1098-4.
  - *Ohio v. Alfieri—Road Rage.* ISBN 0-7668-1099-2.
  - *Flynn v. Goldman Sachs—Fired on Wall Street: A Case of Sex Discrimination?* ISBN 0-7668-1096-8.
  - *Dodd v. Dodd: Religion and Child Custody in Conflict.* ISBN 0-7668-1094-1.
  - *Fentress v. Eli Lilly & Co., et al—Prozac on Trial.* ISBN 0-7668-1095-X.
  - *In RE Custody of Baby Girl Clausen—Child of Mine: The Fight for Baby Jessica.* ISBN 0-7668-1097-6.

- **West's Paralegal Video Library** includes these videos, available at no charge to qualified adopters:
  - *The Drama of the Law II: Paralegal Issues Video.* ISBN 0-314-07088-5.
  - *I Never Said I Was a Lawyer Paralegal Ethics Video.* ISBN 0-314-08049-X.

> Please note that Internet resources are time-sensitive, and URL addresses may often change or be deleted.

Contact us at westlegalstudies@delmar.com

About the Author

Stephanie Delaney is an attorney, instructor, and technology trainer. She earned her Law degree from the University of San Diego School of Law and also holds a Master's degree in Environmental Law from Vermont Law School. She has taught paralegals legal research, both in the classroom and over the Internet, for several years. Her down-to-earth approach to legal research has made her a favorite workshop presenter of the Washington State Bar Association and other clients.

Acknowledgments

Thanks to Pat Bille for encouraging me to write this text and for supporting me in difficult times. I owe a huge thank-you to my mom, Winona Delaney, and to Gavin Smith for voluntarily reading every word of my drafts and for making great suggestions for change. Thanks also to my Summer 2000 Legal 282 class who helped test the concepts. I want to particularly thank students Rinda Evans, Erich Hahn, Bob Jones, and Bobbie Riddle. Thanks to Dr. Joe Mills for the cartoon art. Finally, I would like to thank the following reviewers for their valuable feedback:

Hank Arnold
Aiken Technical College, GA

Eli Bortman
Suffolk University, MA

Dora Dye
City College of San Francisco, CA

Roger Hollands
Ball State University, IN

Luci Hoover
Rockford Business College, IL

Lise Hunter
NYC Technical Center, NY

Jill Jasperson
Utah Valley State College, UT

Sarah Hall Kaufman
Meredith College, NC

Jana Levinstein
American Institute for Paralegal Studies, VA

Brian McCully
Fresno City College, CA

Stephanie Delaney

How to Use This Text

Welcome to *Electronic Legal Research: An Integrated Approach.* The purpose of this book is to introduce you to the process of researching law using electronic (computer-based) sources.

Researching is the process of identifying an issue and then finding relevant information to address that issue. For hundreds of years, this meant scanning through paper indexes to find answers contained in books on library shelves. While this type of search still has its place, the advent of computers brought us new, faster ways to find answers to questions.

Information traditionally stored in books is now frequently stored in computer databases. The advantage here is that computer databases can be searched in seconds, rather than the hours that a traditional search can take. If you ask the right question, the answer you want will pop up on your computer screen in a fraction of the time needed to find the same information in books.

Of course, every technology has its drawbacks. If you do not ask just the right question, the computer database search can return too much information—hundreds of pages of useless responses with a few lines of good information mixed in. Alternately, a computer search could bring back too few answers, even when you are confident that more information is out there.

This text shows you how to ask the right questions of the right databases so that you can do effective legal research using computer resources. This text assumes you have a basic knowledge of how to perform legal research using books. Indeed, this text might supplement your regular legal research text. Since most electronic versions of legal resources are based on the books that they come from, understanding how to research using books first is essential. If you are unclear on how to do a specific type of research using books, refer to your main legal research text.

This text begins with Part One, which explains How to Search. Chapters 1 and 2 explain the basics of searching computer databases using effective search questions, or *queries.* These chapters also give you some general query-forming strategies. Chapters 3 and 4 explain how to apply the query strategies to a variety of databases, including Westlaw, Lexis, and the Internet.

Part Two applies the strategies of Part One to specific types of legal research, including statutes, regulations, case law, and secondary sources. The idea is to integrate research strategies with research tools. When this happens, you can decide effectively where to look for the information you want and know exactly how to get it.

Both Parts One and Two include helpful charts and worksheets to make organizing your research easier. Several worksheets are duplicated in different chapters so that you can fill in the information specific to the current chapter.

This text takes a critical thinking approach to learning. What that means to you is that the book does not give you all the answers. Rather, this text strives to give you the information you need to come up with your own answers. For instance, instead of telling you that a certain Web site is the best for legal research, this text tells you what elements make a good Web site and lets you draw your own intelligent conclusions.

Each chapter has a Guided Exercise that takes you through the process of solving a research process step by step. These exercises help you figure out how to really do the problems and to identify typical mistakes. When going through the chapter, do not just read the Guided Exercise; work it through at your computer; do each step. If you run into trouble, write your questions and take them to your instructor. This helps you learn the material more quickly and easily.

A Web page supplements this text. The Web page has links to information referenced in the chapters, as well as additional exercises for extra help if information does not make sense the first time around. The field of electronic legal research is changing rapidly, and the Web page is designed to help you keep current.

Each chapter of the text builds on previous sections, providing you an integrated approach to database searching. When you finish the text, you should have the confidence to search any electronic database with success.

How to Search

1

Basic Electronic Searching

Chapter Objectives

- **Learn general concepts of using electronic tools:** Using electronic tools to do legal research is not as hard as you might think.
- **Understand Boolean searching:** Boolean logic underlies almost every database of legal information. When you understand how it works, you'll realize that all electronic searching is the same.
- **Use Boolean operators:** Three short words—*AND*, *NOT* and *OR*—are the cornerstones of electronic research.
- **Use other operators:** Proximity and phrase searches and wildcard operators can narrow or expand basic searches, allowing you to craft more concise queries.

On the Web
- Annotated web links leading you to:
  - Information on George Boole
  - More information on Boolean operators
- Exercises for additional help

Electronic Legal Research

Research
looking through
information to find the
answer to a question.

Research is the process of looking through information to find the answer to a question. When you first learn to do traditional legal research, you typically learn various skills separately. You learn to research using digests, popular names tables, or keyword indexes. Over time, you realize what makes legal research complicated: Most sources require slightly different searching strategies.

Electronic research
looking for answers to
questions using computer
databases of information.

   Electronic research is similar, except that you look for answers in computer databases. You generally learn to use resources like Lexis or Westlaw, CD Law or Loislaw. You realize that research using the electronic sources is, like using traditional resources, complicated by differences between programs. You may learn to use one form of electronic legal research really well and then avoid research tools that you did not learn in school.

   You do not need to work that way. In fact, you may be surprised to learn that electronic searching is basically the same from product to product. One factor that unifies electronic searching is the method of searching known as Boolean searching. Once you focus on similarities rather than the differences, electronic legal research suddenly becomes much easier.

Overview of Boolean Searching

Boolean searching is based on the logical structures of algebra first put together by a British man named George Boole in 1847.[1] But, do not let its math basis scare you; Boolean searching is pretty simple to understand. When you search for information electronically, you are generally searching for information stored in some kind of **database**, an organized collection of information. You want to search the database and pull out the individual items relevant to your needs. The logic of Boolean searching lets you do that.

Database
organized collection of
information, searchable
by keyword.

Basic Boolean Operators

Boolean operator
special words used to
connect search terms
when searching a
database.

Connector
see Boolean operator.

You form Boolean search queries using basic words—*AND, OR, NOT*—to determine whether a query, or question, is true or false. Using those simple words, known as **Boolean operators** or **connectors**, you can join search terms in ways that let you to search the database and find the documents that you want. For example, suppose you are curious about Burger King's recall of its Pokéballs.[2] A few years ago the fast-food chain gave out Pokéballs with its kids' meals. After a short time, the company found that the toys were dangerous for children under three and recalled the toys. You determine that product liability is an issue here, and you want more information. (Chapter 2 describes how to identify an issue if you do not know the relevant area of law.)

   To find the information, you can use the Boolean search operators to work in a basic query.

OR

The most basic Boolean search operator is OR. Most search tools default to OR. The **default operator** is the Boolean operator search tools automatically use when a query contains words without connectors between them.

Using OR to begin your product liability search, you could create a query that looks like this:

Product OR liability

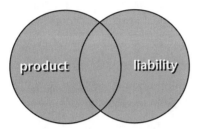

Figure 1-1: Venn diagram illustrating how the Boolean operator OR works.

A search tool answers a query like that in three steps:

1. It looks for every document containing the word *product*.
2. It looks for every document containing the word *liability*.
3. It presents you with a list of all these documents.

The results of that search should be documents on product liability. However, the results might also include contract documents on *product* warranties or environmental cases on strict *liability*. As you can see, you might waste a long time reviewing irrelevant results.

AND

When you search, you generally want all words in your query to appear in the search results. To make that happen, use the popular AND operator. In our product liability search, a query using AND might look like this:

Product AND liability

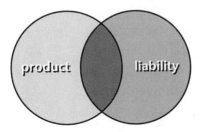

Figure 1-2: Venn diagram illustrating how AND works. The darkest shaded area indicates the results.

A search tool answers a query using these terms in three steps:

1. It looks for every document containing the word *product*.
2. It looks for every document containg the word *liability*.
3. It selects documents that contain both *product* and *liability*.

The results of that query are much better than the results of the OR query. However, the results might still include lots of documents that you do not want.

Imagine that your search brings you dozens of documents on silicone breast implants, which have been the subject of quite a bit of product liability litigation. However, since you are not interested in that topic, you want to omit these documents from the results. This is the perfect opportunity to use the NOT operator.

NOT

The NOT operator is a great way to exclude documents you know will be irrelevant. So, you could try a search like this:

> Product AND liability NOT implant

To conduct this search, a search tool performs four steps:

1. It looks for every document containing the word *product*.
2. It looks for every document containing the word *liability*.
3. It selects documents containing both the words *product* and *liability*.
4. It omits documents containing the word *implant* when it presents the results.

You do not always know which documents to omit before you start your search. However, if you start a search and then see a pattern in the irrelevant documents retrieved, you can use the handy NOT operator to modify your search and narrow your results. Note that you do not need to omit the entire phrase "silicone breast implant," since the words generally come together as a phrase. You could use any of the three words in your NOT query to get similar results.

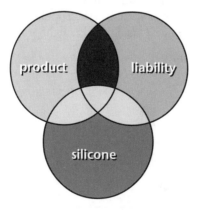

Figure 1-3: Venn diagram illustrating how NOT works. The darkest shaded area indicates the results.

The basic Boolean search operators are the cornerstones of every electronic database, legal or non-legal. A clear understanding of these operators dramatically improves your research effectiveness.

Guided Exercise

This exercise takes you step by step through the process of forming a basic query using the Boolean operators AND, OR, and NOT. This exercise will introduce you to the process of query formation. Chapter 2 covers query formation in greater detail.

Our client, the City of Nearwater, wants to build a boardwalk along the seaside to promote tourism in its waterfront area. Nearwater purchased nearly every lot it needs to complete the project, but one homeowner refuses to sell. Nearwater asks us how it can use its power of imminent domain[3] to acquire the property.

Keyword
term selected to find relevant documents in a database.

1. **Select keywords.** The first step in our query-forming process is to identify **keywords**, those words that help you to find the answer to your question. When selecting keywords, you want to try to (a) identify major legal themes and (b) identify specific information to narrow the search. In our example, the major legal theme is imminent domain. For a more specific search term, we might want to use a word related to water, since this action is taking place near the water.

2. **Select Boolean search operators**. After you choose your keywords, you need to join them using Boolean search operators. In our example, we might want to try

imminent AND *domain* AND *waterfront* OR *seaside*

In this example, we could build the query without the OR operator and obtain results. However, including common alternative words will broaden our search and let us see whether one word is used rather than the other in the legal context. If your search is not producing satisfactory results, using alternative search terms and the OR operator can help you progress.

Exercise 1-1

Practice using the basic search operators by doing Exercise 1-1 at the end of the chapter.

Other Useful Operators

You learned about the basic search operators AND, OR, and NOT—these operators are the foundation of your search. This section introduces other Boolean search terms that will make your search more targeted and accurate.

Proximity Searching

As you learned from the product liability search in the previous section, you could easily do a search resulting in documents where the word *product* appeared on one page and the word *liability* appeared 10 pages later in a different context. To avoid such results, do a **proximity search**. A proximity search often indicated with the search operator **NEAR**, requires that your search terms be relatively close together, usually within 10 to 25 words of each other. Each search tool has its own default number for proximity. You can determine the default number by looking at the Help section of the database. Using NEAR can really improve the relevance of your search results.

Proximity search

searching a database for search terms close to each other, usually within 10 to 25 words of each other. This is often indicated with the Boolean operator NEAR.

HELP!

Every search tool has a Help section. Some Help sections are better than others, but you should always read the Help section first when you try a new search tool. The Help section orients you to how Boolean operators work in that search tool and what the default operator is. It may also give you wonderful tips on how to search that database successfully.

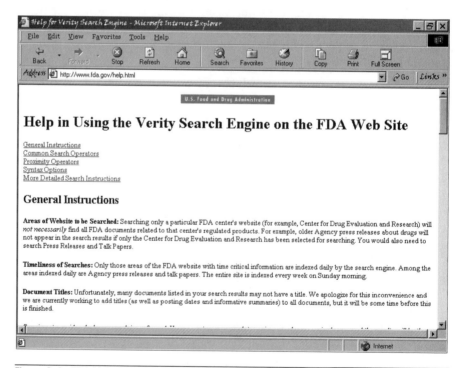

Figure 1-4: FDA Help. Most search engines have sections on how to use them efficiently. *From: www.fda.gov.*

Proximity searching does not guarantee that phrases like *product liability* would appear in the context you want. However, queries like

> Product NEAR liability
> Liability NEAR pokeball

do increase the likelihood that your search returns relevant responses.

You can also conduct proximity searching with the operator **/n**. For our product liability query, you might try:

> Product /5 liability

This query requires that the word *product* occurs within five words of the word *liability*. So, the /n directs the search tool to find your words within a certain number (n) of words of each other. The *n* signifies the number of words you want for the proximity.

Phrase Searching

Phrase search

searching a database for an exact phrase, with the search terms right next to each other. Quotation marks or parentheses often surround the phrase.

With our Pokéball scenario, finding the words *product* and *liability* right next to each other would really be useful. A **phrase search** lets you find two or more consecutive words. For phrase searching, most databases require that you use quotation marks or parentheses around the phrase:

> "product liability"
> (product liability)

Stopwords

words that search tools ignore because they appear too frequently. Examples include the words *the*, *of* and *a*.

Phrase searching brings results with the words next to each other in any order. Also, phrase searching generally finds plural words (*products*, *liabilities*). However, it ignores what researchers call **stopwords** (*a*, *the*, *to*, *of*, *as*, and the like). So, a phrase search of *product liability* might find a sentence like this:

> *The court found the plaintiff's distress to be the **product** of the **liability** she bore due to her negligence.*

The search ignores stopwords *of* and *the*.

Stopwords

When executing a search, search tools ignore stopwords because they occur so frequently, they would slow the search or give irrelevant results. Listed in the Help section of many search tools, stopwords generally include the following:

◆ **articles** (*a*, *an*, *the*)

◆ **pronouns** (*his*, *her*, *their*)

◆ **adjectives** (*very*, *many*, *best*)

◆ **prepositions** (*of*, *in*, *at*)

◆ **Boolean search operators** (AND, OR, NOT, NEAR)

The existence of stopwords can pose problems at times. For example, if you search for information on Vitamin A, most search tools only find the word *vitamin*, since *A* is a stopword. Even if you search for the phrase *Vitamin A*, the search tool ignores the letter *A*. You might be able to work around that limitation by using words commonly associated with your word or phrase. For example, liver and milk are good sources of Vitamin A. Try this search:

     Vitamin NEAR milk OR liver

Phrase searching also presents a danger that can sabotage the unwary researcher's search. It is possible to make your search too specific, so you must be very careful what you ask for in a phrase search query. In our Pokéball scenario, you might search for a phrase like:

> "Product liability for Burger King Pokeballs"

This query only results in sentences that include our exact phrase. It only finds sentences that contain all the phrase words right next to each other. Thus, a document with a sentence like:

> *"The court found that the product liability for the toys rested with the product manufacturer."*

might not appear as a query result, since the words *Burger King* and *Pokéball* are not present. This sentence is very relevant to our search, yet it would not appear in our search results. As you can see, overly specific phrase searching might eliminate perfectly valid results. Phrase searching is a wonderful and valuable tool, but be sure to use it with caution. The next chapter includes more about search strategies.

Wildcard Operators

Searching a database is a fairly precise activity. As you may have experienced, search tools look for exactly what you ask for, misspellings and all. If you are not sure how to spell a word or if the word has several forms (like *liability* or *liable*), you can use wildcard operators to look for alternatives. Depending on the search tool used, an exclamation point (!), question mark (?), or asterisk (*) represents a wildcard operator, also known as a root expander. The **wildcard operator** lets you use the root of the word to find any words with that root. For example:

Wildcard operator
symbol used to find variations of a search term. Sometimes called a root expander.

     Liab!
     Child!

The first example finds both the words *liability* and *liable*. The second finds both the words like *child, children, childish, childlike*, and so on.

Stemming
process in which a database automatically looks for common variations of a word, most commonly its plural form.

Search tools often assume that you want the most common variations of your search terms to appear in your results. This process is known as stemming. **Stemming** is basically the automatic inclusion of a wildcard operator. For example, if you enter the word *ball*, stemming automatically looks for the word *balls*. Many databases perform stemming automatically, eliminating the need to include special operators or additional search operators. However, unlike the wildcard operators, stemming only looks for the most common variations of a word, generally its plural form. To find other forms of the word, like the word *childlike* above, use the wildcard operators. Take a quick look at the Help section of your database to learn whether stemming happens automatically and if so, what kind of stemming the search tool does.

If your search tool offers stemming and also allows wildcard operators, you can use the two together or separately to obtain the results you want. If you are just looking for the plural of your word, use stemming alone. If you are looking for more complex variations of your word, like *childlike*, use the wildcard operator.

In addition to using a wildcard operator to replace word endings, you can use a wildcard operator to replace specific letters within a word. Often represented by an asterisk or question mark, this wildcard operator can come in handy when you are uncertain of a spelling or when you want to include several variations of the word. For example:

> Wom*n

finds documents containing the words *woman, women, womyn,* and so on. Many databases let you use more than one wildcard at a time. For example:

> *ffect!

finds the words *affect, effect, effecting, affection,* and so on. Using wildcard operators is a great way to increase the scope of your search.

Exercise 1-2   Practice using all of the Boolean search operators by answering the questions in Exercise 1-2 at the end of the chapter.

SUMMARY

Now you know about the basic tools that nearly every database uses to facilitate your search for information. Whether you use Westlaw or Lexis, the Internet or a court records database, you will use some combination of these tools:

- **Boolean operators:** AND, OR, NOT
- **proximity search:** NEAR, W/n
- **phrase search:** quotation marks or parentheses
- **word variations:** wildcard operators, like asterisk (*), exclamation point (!), or question mark (?); and also automatic stemming.

Throughout this text, we will explore different databases. As we do, we will first explore how the database uses these operators. As you encounter new databases in your research, whether it is legal research or not, you can make the process of searching much easier if you look in Help and spend a few moments reviewing how each database uses these simple and constant tools.

Notes

1. Information on George Boole gathered from *www.britannica.com*.
2. "Burger King voluntarily recalls Pokémon balls," December 27, 1999. *http://www.burgerking.com/company/press_releases/12_27_99.htm*
3. Imminent domain is the power of a government entity to acquire private property for a public purpose. The government must pay the landowner fair value for the property.

EXERCISES

Exercise 1-1

Read the following scenarios. Identify keywords and then try to join the keywords using Boolean search operators. Do not try to create perfect queries; The next chapter discusses query formation in detail.

1. Dick wrote and published a truthful editorial about Jane's bad housekeeping. Jane wants to sue for slander.

2. Lars sold stock for a company that did not exist. Is he liable for fraud?

3. Henry delivered the fresh flowers a day late for Susan's wedding. She had a contract that specified the delivery date, and time was of the essence. What kind of damages could Susan collect for the breach of contact?

4. Zora died and left her entire estate to her cat, Mr. Pipo. Was the will valid?

5. Badco regularly refused to hire female workers over age 24. Is Badco liable for sex discrimination?

Exercise 1-2

Rewrite your queries from Exercise 1-1, adding phrase searching, proximity searching, and wild-card operators.

Chapter Review Exercises

Read the questions below. Identify the keywords and join them using the search operators explained in this chapter.

1. MeanCredit, Inc. regularly threatens relatives of people who have not paid their bills. Is the company liable for intentional infliction of emotional distress?

2. Bang's cat regularly enters Bing's yard to use the garden as a litter box. Bing is mad and wants to sue Bang. Is Bang liable for the tort of trespass?

3. Last month, Brad failed to pay rent for his apartment. Instead, he used the rent money to make needed repairs to the apartment. Maria, his landlady, has threatened to evict Brad, but he claims the law is on his side, since without the repairs, the apartment is unsafe. Can Maria legally evict Brad?

4. Listening to the radio, Melody, a songwriter, heard a famous pop star singing one of her songs. Melody looked into it and discovered that Off Note Records found her song on the Internet and used the song without her permission. Can Melody sue for copyright infringement?

5. Hammand, a Muslim, was selected to give the opening prayer next month at the beginning of a football game sponsored by his public school. He wants to say a Muslim prayer, noting that the school permits Christian students to offer their prayers before football games. The school tells Hammand that he must choose a Christian prayer. He wonders what his rights are under the Freedom of Religion clause of the United States Constitution.

Boolean Search Operators

Operator Type	*Terms*
Basic Boolean Operators	**AND**—All joined terms appear in each document.
	NOT—Joined term does not appear in the document.
	OR—At least one joined term appears in the document.
Proximity Search	**NEAR**—Joined terms appear within a certain number of words of each other.
	W/n—Joined term appears within the specified number (n) of words of each other.
Phrase Search	**Quotation marks " "**—All terms within the marks appear together in the document.
	Parentheses ( )—All terms within the marks appear together in the document.
Word Variations (wildcard)	**Asterisk ***—Depending on the database, substitutes for a letter or series of letters in the term.
	Exclamation point !—Depending on the database, substitutes for a letter or series of letters in the term.
	Question mark ?—Depending on the database, substitutes for a letter or series of letters in the term.

Joined terms refers to words, phrases, or keywords, connected by the search operator.

2

Query Formation Strategy

Chapter Objectives

- **Query Formation Strategy:** You are asked to go and find that document—but how do you do it? What keywords should you use, and how should you put them together? In this chapter, you learn the answers to these questions.

- **The Five Questions:** This simple research strategy helps you form effective queries to get the results you want every time.

- **Troubleshoot queries:** Not finding what you want? You learn how to get your search back on track.

On the Web

- Annotated links leading you to:
  - More information on Query Formation
  - More information on Search Strategies
- Exercises for additional help

Introduction to Queries

When you do electronic legal research, you actually extract information from computer databases. Fortunately, the process of searching computer databases is more or less the same, regardless of which database you use. This section provides an overview of that process.

Query
request to a database for information it contains, using keywords joined by connectors.

To search a computer database, you begin by constructing a query. A **query** is a list of words, or search terms, that tells the computer what you want to find. For example, you might type the words *product liability* to tell the computer to find documents on product liability. However, as we saw in Chapter 1, such searches might find several documents about products, dozens of documents about liability, and only a few documents that actually discuss product liability.

Therefore, to create a good query, you must be more specific. Computer databases provide methods for being specific using the Boolean search operators. As discussed in Chapter 1, a Boolean search operator is just a word, such as *AND*, *OR*, or *NOT*, that tells the computer database how you want the query to link your search terms. Do you want documents containing the words *product* OR *liability*, or just documents containing the words *product* AND *liability*?

Boolean search operators are key players in building a good query. Traditionally, mastering the art of crafting the perfect query has been very difficult. Many users become discouraged with their inability to create a good query and thus feel constantly frustrated when trying to search for information.

Natural language searching
ability to query a database in the same way that you question a person, without using Boolean operators.

To overcome this frustration, many databases have what is known as natural language searching. **Natural language searching** lets you ask the database your question in the same way that you ask a person, without using the rather unnatural Boolean search operators. For example, you might ask:

Is Burger King liable for harm suffered by small children who used the Pokeball?

Behind the scenes, the natural language program in the database takes your question, analyzes it, and then translates it into a Boolean search. The translated query might look like this:

"Burger King" /5 liable AND /5 harm AND children OR Pokeball

The database runs the translated Boolean search without your worrying about what operators to use. On the surface, natural language searching is great. However, you'll soon find that natural language searches are not as targeted as Boolean searches you create yourself; they can yield a significant number of irrelevant results. That's because the database is guessing what you want to find, and it sometimes guesses wrong.

Skilled Boolean searching has been and is likely to continue to be the most efficient method of searching. In addition, Boolean searching is appropriate for nearly every kind of database. Once you become comfortable with Boolean searching, you can easily search most databases. On the other hand, few databases can perform natural language searching. So this chapter focuses on building those skills necessary to craft a universally good query using Boolean search operators.

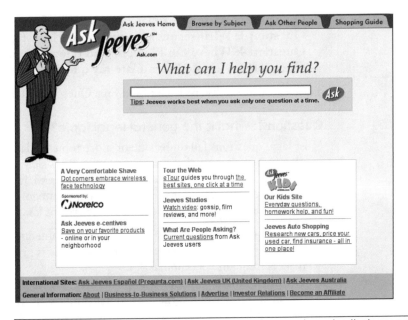

Figure 2-1: Search screen for Ask Jeeves, a popular search engine that uses natural language searching. *From the* Ask Jeeves *Web Page, www.ask.com. Used with permission of* Ask Jeeves Inc. *All rights reserved.*

First, you need a strategy. You might find this initial step of legal research hard to remember, because when you have something to research, you want to get right to it. You long to go straight to the books or to log onto Lexis or Westlaw quickly and start searching. But, you immediately benefit from taking your time and creating a well crafted query. A few minutes spent thinking about what you want to find and where to find it is time well spent. Students are frequently frustrated because they are not sure where to start a research project. The query formation strategy should take care of that, helping you know where to begin and how to move forward.

This text emphasizes the use of a **research strategy**, a plan that makes you think about the task ahead. The research strategy is very important in facilitating the effective research process. Forming a good query without it is difficult. The research strategy might seem a bit cumbersome at first, but after a while this planning process becomes second nature. Also, keep in mind that the same strategy works for every kind of research, legal or non-legal, with computers or with books.

A Query Formation Strategy

You can use any strategy that seems to work for you; the one presented here works well for many students. Once you have a question that you need to research, ask yourself the following **Five Questions** to find potential answers.

Question 1: What is the general legal topic?

Research Strategy
plan created to make the researcher think about the research to be done, which thus makes the process more effective. The plan usually includes a determination of relevant law and the best keywords.

Five Questions
a research strategy.

Question 2: What type of law am I looking for?
Question 3: What secondary sources do I investigate?
Question 4: Where can I look to find relevant information?
Question 5: How do I formulate my query?

The next sections discuss each of the Five Questions individually.

Question 1: What is the general legal topic?

Most legal questions fall under one or more topics of law. Therefore, answering this first question relies a great deal on your basic knowledge of the law. If you look at a question and have absolutely no idea what area of law it is, follow these very general guidelines about some major categories of law. Keep in mind that your issues may involve more than one area of law.

- **Civil or criminal:** Is someone trying to sue someone else? If so, you know the area of law is civil, not criminal. If the state is prosecuting someone, the issue is frequently a criminal one.
- **Criminal law:** Is someone facing jail time? Was a crime committed? Is a prosecutor involved? Is the government the plaintiff? Are police involved? If so, you might be looking at a criminal law issue.
- **Civil procedures:** Some issues fall ouside the area of substantive law and concern the legal procedures of court. Is there a question about discovery? About the method or timing of documents filed? If you have a civil procedure issue, remember to refer to the appropriate procedural statute or court rules for more information.
- **Contracts:** Was there an express (written or spoken) agreement between the parties? If so, the issue is probably one of contract law. If the two parties are businesses, the issue may be one of commercial law involving the Uniform Commercial Code.
- **Property:** The several categories of property include real, personal, and intellectual property.
  - **Real property:** Does the question regard the transfer of land from one to another? That is real property law. Does it regard how one uses his or her land? That may be zoning and land use law. It could also be about environmental law, which, from a property standpoint, deals primarily with soil contamination and other pollution.
  - **Intellectual property:** Issues of copyrights, patents, and trademarks fall within this category. If your issue concerns rights associated with the creation of books, music, Web pages, new inventions, art, symbols, and the like, your issue may involve the area of intellectual property.
- **Torts:** Has one person harmed another in a noncriminal way? Trespass, fraud, mental duress, auto accidents, slips and falls, and other personal injuries are addressed by tort law. Tort law also includes product liability, where a consumer product harms someone. That is the case in our Pokéball scenario.
- **Family law:** Does the issue involve marriage and divorce? Children's issues like child custody, child support, and adoption are all within this category as well.

If, after looking at these general guidelines, you still have no idea of the area of law involved, try a dictionary for unfamiliar words or simply ask someone. Once you know the general area of law, you can go to the next question.

Figure 2-2: Protecting intellectual property is always important. *Illustration by Joe Mills. Reprinted with permission. All rights reserved.*

Question 2: What type of law am I looking for?

Does state or federal law involve this topic? Would a statute, regulation, or case law discuss it? To answer this question, you need a good idea of what types of issues state or federal law covers. One student looking for a divorce statute in the United States Code became very frustrated. She could not find any of the laws she expected, because state law, not federal law, covers most family law issues, including divorce. Knowing whether the relevant law is state, federal, or both assists you in searching successfully.

State law generally regulates topics like criminal law, family law, contracts, estate planning, and property. Federal law regulates topics dealing with federal laws and the United States Constitution. Some areas, like administrative law and environmental law, may go either way, depending on the parties and the subject involved. Look carefully at any government agency involved—is it a state or federal agency? That answer can give you a good indication of whether state or federal law is involved.

Next, you need to determine whether the relevant law is a statute, regulation, court case, or some combination of all these. Remember, statutes tend to be broad pronouncements of law, regulations are more detailed, and cases apply facts to the law in specific situations. If you are uncertain what kind of law to search, try looking for relevant cases, since cases often lead you to other relevant law. Keep in mind that very current issues may not have any cases **on point**. Cases take a while to work their way through the system to the appellate level, where most cases must arrive before they are reported. Remember that this question is important in helping you narrow your search. If you are not sure about the

On point
a case which specifically addresses some or all of an issue.

kind of law involved, try looking at some secondary sources mentioned in Question 3. They might help you find the answer.

Question 3: What secondary sources do I investigate?

There are hundreds of secondary sources are out there. Often starting with the basics—a legal dictionary or a legal encyclopedia—is best. A quick search of these sources for your key terms or ideas helps you understand what you are researching and gives you a big-picture overview of the topic. It also gives you additional keywords and generally facilitates your research. Hornbooks and practice books are also useful in getting a good grounding in relevant law. Unless you are really pressed for time, spending twenty or thirty minutes familiarizing yourself with the area of law you are researching saves lots of time and effort later.

Question 4: Where can I look to find relevant information?

In electronic legal research, you generally choose to search a variety of databases. One might have information on federal statutes, another might contain all federal case law, and a third might combine the two kinds of information. In addition, you might have access to several different sources of information, for example, the Internet, Westlaw, a local product like CD Law, and specialized desk books. Deciding which resource or combination of resources to start with is part of a good strategy.

Be specific when answering this question. Rather than generally determining to use the Internet, you should instead brainstorm about which specific Web sites to use or which specific search engine to use to find the Web sites. Rather than simply deciding to use Westlaw, determine which directory and specific file to start in. This step further helps to focus your search and obtain the results you want. If you do not know right away where to start, take a moment to try to think it through. In any case, try to be as specific as possible.

Question 5: How do I formulate my query?

At this point, you begin determining exactly how to ask for the information you want to find. What keywords will you use? How will you put them together? Which combinations of Boolean search operators will yield the best results? Strategizing ahead of time about how you to put your query together can help you focus on this most frustrating step of searching.

Keep one important thing in mind: Once you form a query, do not become too attached to it. If you devise a query you like, try it a few times to see what kind of results you get. If you do not get the results you want, do not be afraid to tweak the query a little or toss it altogether and try something else.

Answering this query construction question also requires you to focus on your keywords. The first four questions help lead you to keywords, but the actual process of selecting the best keywords is an art that you learn over time. Here are some general hints:

Issue statement
legal question that research aims to answer.

- **Put your question into an issue statement.** This works best when you use the whether/when format. For example, in the last chapter, we wanted to know about Burger King's liability for the Pokéball. An issue question in the whether/when format might read:

Whether Burger King is liable for injuries caused by the Pokéball **when** it distributed the balls without age appropriate warnings?

Simply formulating the issue statement helps you organize your thoughts. The first part of the issue statement (whether) focuses on the broader issue, in this case, liability for injury. The second part of the statement (when) focuses on the particular, in this case, distribution of the toys without appropriate warning. In other words, your question begins a process of analysis in which you combine the legal rule with the important facts of the matter.

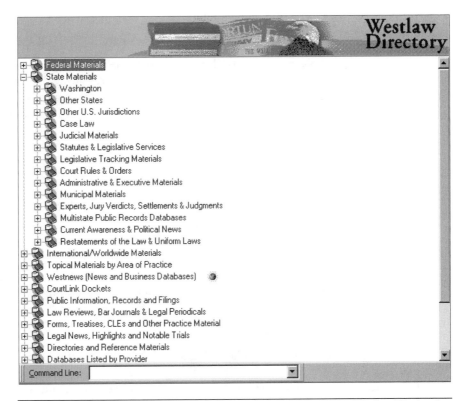

Figure 2-3: Westlaw makes selecting the right directory easy. *From Westlaw Westmate. Used with permission of West Group. All rights reserved.*

- **Avoid overly fact-specific words.** A query for relevant cases on the Burger King matter that includes the words *Burger King* and *Pokéball* would probably not produce any results. The same query might work great for fact-specific media searches, but given the more general nature of legal authorities, such words probably cannot yield successful results. So, focus instead on general legal principles, in this case, product liability.

- **Be careful with statutes.** Statutes often use specific legal words with specific legal meanings. For example, in some states, marriages are dissolved. If you search these states' statutory law for the term *divorce*, you would have no luck, since all these statutes use the word *dissolution* instead. If you are uncertain of the specific word the statutes use, try guessing, using a variety of words with the OR operator. (Guessing is a perfectly legitimate search tactic!) If that doesn't work, try a keyword search of cases to see if any refer to the statute. Courts often use the more common words in their decisions, especially in the statement of facts.

The query construction phase of your planning is the time you need to think about which combination of Boolean operators to use. Sometimes simple searches get you where you want to go; more often you will want to combine operators to obtain the best results. If you are looking for a news story on the Pokéball matter, you might try a query like this:

"Burger King" AND "product liability" NEAR Pokéball

This combination of keywords and Boolean operators starts you on the path to finding the answer to your question. After reviewing the results, you can determine if the query needs tweaking or if you found what you wanted on your first try.

The art of putting together a query is emphasized throughout this text. It is the primary skill that separates the effective researcher from the ineffective one. Once you master it, you improve your ability to find just what you are looking for and become more comfortable about actually finding it.

Guided Exercise

The following guided exercise leads you through the process of using the Five Questions.

Remember the Pokéball example from Chapter 1? Burger King recalled the small Pokémon balls distributed with its kids' meals after learning that the toys could endanger children under three. Your client wants to sue Burger King for injury her five-year old child suffered because of the Pokémon ball. Can she prevail? Ask the Five Questions to lay the foundation for your search.

Question 1: What is the general legal topic? Answering this question should be simple, since we already discussed product liability as the type of law. Product liability is a section of tort law, which applies to injuries that require compensation. Even if you did not immediately narrow the choice to product liability, you may have guessed that it is a tort. The secondary source helps you get to the more specific area of product liability.

Question 2: What kind of law am I looking for? Generally, common law addresses tort law. However, several statutes at both the state and federal level also address some product liability issues through consumer protection laws. So, choosing which way to go could be a toss-up. If after some thought, you cannot determine the answer to this question (or any of the Five Questions) move ahead to the next question. This research strategy aims to help you in the research process, not stop you before you even get going!

Question 3: What secondary sources do I investigate? Be specific when answering this question. As you try to lay your foundation for understanding the issue, where should you look? Starting with a legal dictionary or a legal encyclopedia is always good, especially if you have trouble answering Questions One and Two. After that, think about whether law review articles might cover the subject. Perhaps the general news media is a good source of information. If the matter involves an industry, try industry newsletters or other publications. Be specific here—doing so makes everything else fall into place more easily.

For our Pokéball case, the general media is a good source of specific information about the facts of this case. Law review articles on product liability can likely yield some good results as well.

Question 4: Where can I look for relevant information? Questions One through Three are really foundation questions that help you get enough information to move forward. Question Four, however, is a question of strategy. Where do you begin your search? On the Internet? On a paid legal database? If so, which directory and specific file can provide the best information? Perhaps you want to start with a book, like a dictionary.

In our case, the Pokéball issue received quite a bit of news coverage, so a general Internet search is a good way to get some background information. When you look for law review articles on product liability, try the paid legal database and look in specific directories on product liability or torts.

Question 5: How do I formulate my query? After you answer this final question, you can start your search. Keep in mind that over the course of your research, you probably need to use several different queries to find information in the same resource and certainly several different queries to find information in different resources. Since your queries will vary, you may wonder: Why bother to answer this question? Well, the reason is it provides the opportunity to focus. Simply taking a moment to focus on keywords and phrases and to think about Boolean tools allows you the time to formulate a really good query. The process is far more efficient than guessing as you go along.

Do not become too attached to your query! In fact, you probably want to create several alternative queries before beginning your research, especially if you use paid legal databases. If the first query does not work, you can quickly and easily try the next one.

If your query does not work, check to make sure you are looking in the right place. If you are looking in the right place, try one of your alternate queries. Sometimes, modifying Boolean search terms is all you need to do. If you get too many results, try narrowing your results with a date restriction or more specific database.

For the Pokéball case, the sample query discussed earlier in the chapter might work well:

"Burger King" AND "product liability" NEAR pokeball

This is, of course, just a sample formulation. Depending on the type of database you select, the query may or may not be good. Indeed, the value of a query depends completely on where you perform the search. You can ask the best question in the world, but if it's in the wrong place you will not receive useful results.

Query formation is a skill that takes a while to acquire. Like many areas of law, there is no right or wrong way to phrase a query and, unfortunately, no magic formula that always gets you perfect results. Be patient as you learn to form well crafted queries and do not give up. Even the most experienced researchers revise their queries, again and again before they get the results they want.

Narrowing Your Results

It is not uncommon for searches to produce hundreds more results than you can effectively look through. Use the following hints to narrow your search.

- **Limit the dates.** The best search tools permit you to limit your search to documents within certain date ranges. If you are searching for a popular subject, try limiting your results to the current year. If you are looking for a case that you know was decided in the early eighties, try limiting your search to "1979-1986." Each database handles date restrictions differently, so be sure to check Help for the proper format.

- **Select a more specific database.** The more specific your database, the fewer results you will get. For example, to search for an Idaho products liability case, you might select a database with all federal and state cases. The search gets results, but it also yields lots of irrelevant federal cases. Alternately, you could try searching of a database with information on all states. But this would yield results from Indiana as well as Idaho. The most specific database is one with just Idaho cases. So, although all three databases contain the right case, the most specific database makes the right case easier to find.

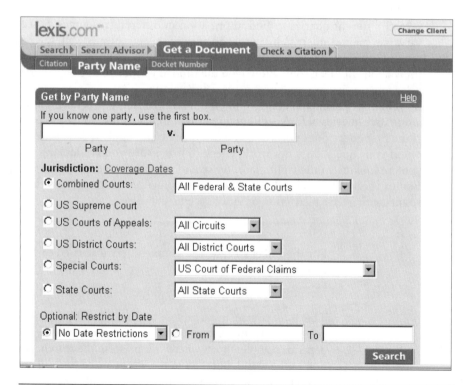

Figure 2-4: At the bottom of the Lexis search screen, you have the option of limiting the date range of your search. *Reprinted with the permission of LEXIS-NEXIS, a division of Reed Elsevier Inc. Lexis-Nexis, Lexis, Nexis, the Information Array logo and lexis.com are registered trademarks of Reed Elsevier Properties Inc. used with the permission of LEXIS-NEXIS.*

♦ **Use phrase or proximity searching.** Take advantage of Boolean tools to limit your search to specific phrases or words close to each other. Searching for

> products AND liability AND Pokeball

produces entirely different results than searching for

> "product liability" NEAR pokeball

Using proximity and phrase searching, you can effectively narrow your results to the documents you want.

<table>
<tr><td>Exercise
2-1</td><td>Practice your query formation skills by answering the questions in Exercise 2-1 at the end of the chapter.</td></tr>
</table>

Query Troubleshooting

Since query formation is a learned skill, in the beginning you can expect to run into some roadblocks. Do not worry—this is normal. If you do not get the results you want from your query, ask yourself the following questions.

- **Did I plan my strategy?** Researchers who are stymied in the research process have often skipped the planning process and thus are not really sure what they are searching for or where they expect to find it. Taking time to think significantly speeds the research process and increases the accuracy of your results.
- **Am I searching in the right place?** The best search query won't yield results from the wrong database. Ask yourself, "Why am I searching this specific database?" If you are not sure, go back to your research strategy. If you began by searching a very specific database, try to broaden your search. If you used restrictions or phrase searching, double-check to make sure you are using these tools correctly. Make sure you are not searching a case database for statutes. If you are searching for statutes, keep in mind that this is one area in which using the right word is essential. Try looking for a statute by finding cases that refer to it, and you can more easily find a statute whose keywords are difficult to determine.
- **Am I using the right words?** Because legal language tends to be obscure, the important task of selecting the correct keywords becomes rather difficult. If you are uncertain of your search terms, consult a legal dictionary or encyclopedia. These valuable secondary sources can help you find the proper phrasing, so you can then find the documents you need. In addition, legal dictionaries and legal encyclopedias often direct researchers to landmark cases that define or explain the word or concept. Quickly Sheparding the referenced landmark case can also help put your research on the right track. **Sheparding**, the process of checking whether a law still applies, can lead you to other cases that reference key sections of the case you search. As a result, you might find even more relevant cases.

Sheparding
generally, the process of checking a law to make sure that it still applies. When Sheparding cases, you may find other relevant cases that refer to yours, this makes Sheparding a good research tool.

- **Do I understand what I am looking for?** Sometimes, you get start on a research project and find just the right case on your first try. Hurray! Unfortunately, if you are not sure what you are looking for, you may keep looking. That's because you do not understand that the case that you have is on point. A basic grasp of the area of law you are searching really assists you in recognizing valid results when you see them. Refer to a legal dictionary or encyclopedia for some background.

- **Am I misusing the phrase operator?** While phrase searching is a great tool for narrowing results, misusing it can result in no results. Try reworking your query using the NEAR or /n operator to broaden your results.

- **Does what I am looking for exist?** If all attempts fail, you may be looking for something that simply does not exist or is not available electronically. Some things to remember:

  - Most state cases do not make it to the case reporters until the cases reach appellate court. You may not find state cases from the trial court level.

  - Writing and publishing law review and journal articles take several months. If you search for very current topics (those that arose within the last two to four months), you may not find them addressed in law review articles. Instead, try searching legal and mainstream newspapers or monthly publications.

  - When researching cutting edge areas of law, like cyberlaw, finding documents that exactly match your issue may be difficult. However, basic legal principles are fairly constant. Thus, if you look for discussions of jurisdiction in cyberspace, traditional cases on jurisdiction can be persuasive, even if they do not specifically focus on cyberlaw.

  - **Did I spell my query words correctly?** An otherwise perfectly constructed query containing a simple spelling error can prevent you from getting the results you expect. Such an error can cause frustration, so double-check your spelling.

Do not become too discouraged when your search does not yield the results you want immediately. Remember that becoming an effective researcher is a process that takes time. Answering these query troubleshooting questions helps you get past many research roadblocks. Use the Query Troubleshooting Worksheet at the end of the chapter as a guide.

SUMMARY

This chapter covers the big issue of how to form an effective query. It looks at a research strategy and explores some troubleshooting questions. Query formation is a learned skill emphasized throughout the book.

Feeling overwhelmed by the task of beginning a new research project is not unusual. Fortunately, using a search strategy can facilitate your task and always give you a place to start. If you take time to use this strategy or another that works well for you, you can perform research faster, more accurately and with less stress.

Notes

1. Susan Rich is author of the *Cartographer's Tongue*, a book of poetry on global travel published by White Pine Press.

EXERCISES

Exercise 2-1

Forming issue statements is a helpful, but rather challenging process. Read the following fact scenarios and try to create a whether/when statement for each. Keep in mind that the first part of the statement addresses the law generally and the second part gets at the specifics.

1. Becky wants to buy a house with Diane. They think they want to buy the house as joint tenants, but they are not entirely sure what it means to own real property in joint tenancy.

2. An adoring fan assaulted Susan Rich, the famous poet.[1] Susan learned who did it and wondered if she had any way to sue the fan under civil tort law, aware that cases like hers are usually criminal matters.

3. Carin had been sick for many months, and her doctor told her she only had a day or two left to live. After the doctor left, Carin gave her prized diamond broach to her nurse, Marta, who had cared for her for many months. Carin miraculously survived and was soon in perfect health. She asked Marta to return the gift, and Marta refused. Is there anything Carin can do?

Chapter Review Exercises

Read the following fact scenarios, and answer the Five Questions to plan your search process. The handy Five Questions Worksheet at the end of the chapter can assist you.

1. Greg and Erich entered into an agreement for Erich to buy a classic guitar from Greg for $950. They had no written agreement; the men just shook hands. Greg told Erich that the guitar would be ready in one week. When Erich arrived at the appointed time to get the guitar, Greg decided he did not want to sell. Erich wants to enforce the agreement. Can he?

2. Dastardly Doug decided to rob the home of Sally Sloppy. While in the house, Doug fell on a bicycle in the hall and sprained his ankle. Doug wants to sue Sally for negligence. Can he prevail?

3. Click and Clack buy an old beach house as joint tenants. For many years, the brothers enjoyed the house together. When Click prepared his will, he left his part of the home to his son Clunk. Is his bequest valid?

4. After recovering from the sprained ankle, Dastardly Doug decided to rob a jewelry store. Doug wore a black ski mask but was unarmed. When Doug entered the store, old Mr. Diamond was so horrified that he had a heart attack and died. Can Doug be charged for murder?

5. Ken recently started having stomach problems. He thinks that during surgery five years ago, his doctor left a sponge in his tummy. He wonders if it is too late to sue the doctor for malpractice. Is it?

Worksheet

The Five Questions

A worksheet for initiating research

Question 1: What is the general legal topic?

Hint: Torts? Contracts? Criminal law? Use a dictionary or encyclopedia to get background information and to look up additional keywords.

Answer:

Question 2: What type of law am I looking for?

Hint: State or federal or both? Statute, regulation, case law, or a combination?

Answer:

Question 3: What secondary sources do I investigate?

Hint: Encyclopedia? Law review or journals? Mainstream media? Interest group or agency Web sites?

Answer:

Question 4: Where can I find relevant information?

Hint: Answer this question in detail. Do not simply answer the Internet; include possible Web sites. Do not just answer Lexis; include the library and file.

Answer:

Question 5:   How do I formulate my query?

Hint: Identify keywords and determine the best way to put them together.

Answer:

Worksheet

Query Troubleshooting

A handy reference for resolving research problems

Trouble Shooting Question: Did I plan my strategy?

Comments: Do not skip the planning process! Make sure to take each step of your strategy.

Result of double checking:

Trouble Shooting Question: Am I searching in the right place?

Comments: Make sure that you are using the right database and that the information on it contains is neither too broad nor too narrow for your search.

Result of double checking:

Trouble Shooting Question: Am I using the right words?

Comments: Check your terms and include alternative words with the OR operator. Use legal dictionary to expand possible terms.

Result of double checking:

Trouble Shooting Question: Do I understand what I am looking for?

Comments: Make sure you really understand the question. Use a legal dictionary or encyclopedia for clarification.

Result of double checking:

Trouble Shooting Question: Am I misusing the phrase operator?

Comments: If using a phrase operator, make sure it is not too specific. Rework using proximity search operators.

Result of double checking:

Trouble Shooting Question: Does what I am looking for exist?

Comments: Think about whether the information exists at all or exists electronically where you are looking.

Result of double checking:

Trouble Shooting Question: Did I spell my words correctly?

Comments: Make sure the spelling, spacing, and punctuation in your search term are correct.

Result of double checking:

3

Paid Legal Databases

Chapter Objectives

- **Learn general concepts:** What are paid legal databases? Why do you need them?
- **Explore Westlaw and Lexis:** Everyone in the legal world has heard of these major legal information providers. You will learn to use Boolean search operators in Westlaw and Lexis.
- **Use other paid legal databases:** Loislaw and CD Law are examples of the many smaller electronic legal databases on the market.
- **Begin your research:** A guided exercise helps you practice using a research strategy in your favorite paid legal database.

On the Web

- Annotated links leading you to:
  - Paid legal databases
  - Specific research hints for Westlaw, Lexis, CD Law, and Loislaw
- Exercises for additional help

Introduction

Dozens of **paid legal databases** are on the market today. Everyone recognizes the names *Lexis* and *Westlaw* as the nation's leaders in providing legal information. At the regional level, law offices turn to Premis, CD Law, and similar products. New legal databases are introduced frequently. One example is Loislaw, an Internet-only paid legal database.

You could spend a lot of time trying to master each technology individually and become frustrated every time the product is updated or whenever a new product is introduced. However, such frustration is unnecessary. For most research, the same strategies discussed in Chapter 2 will work to get you the results you want: one strategy, many products. So, whether you use Westlaw or Loislaw, you can find what you are looking for with a minimum expenditure of time and effort.

Please note that this chapter on paid legal databases does not attempt to teach you how to use individual databases. The information providers have excellent training resources of their own; there is no need to reinvent the wheel. Indeed, many information providers offer online tutorials that teach you the basics and introduce the latest innovations.[1] So, rather than teaching you the nuts and bolts of using the databases, this chapter focuses on how to use the strategies introduced in Chapter 2 to work successfully with each database.

Westlaw

Figure 3-1: Westlaw logo. *Reprinted with the permission of West Group.*

Westlaw provides dial-up and Web access to hundreds of legal materials. Its primary source databases include cases, statutes, and regulations from all fifty states, the District of Columbia, and Law from several foreign jurisdictions. Westlaw also includes secondary sources like legal journals, hornbooks, and legal periodicals. In addition, Westlaw provides bill tracking tools (for researching law that has not yet been enacted) and search legislative history (the background of law as it was being created). Westlaw's directories incorporate information from over 5000 news and business databases.[2] Westlaw offers unique services as well, like the KeyCite citation service, which is similar to Shepard's citation service. KeyCite provides legal history and lists citing references to make sure you have good law.

Dial-up connection
using a modem, your
computer can call, or
dial up, another
computer so you
can access the
information there.

Traditionally, researchers accessed Westlaw via a dial-up connection. In a **dial-up connection**, a researcher's computer "dials up," or calls, the Westlaw computer. This requires the researcher to have specific Westlaw software installed and generally restricts the researcher to searching from that computer only or from another computer with Westlaw software installed. However, today more and more Westlaw subscribers access its services through the Internet at Westlaw.com (**www.westlaw.com**). This gives the researcher the flexibility to access Westlaw databases from any computer with an Internet connection and requires no special Westlaw software.

Figure 3-2: Westlaw.com logo. You can access Westlaw's databases over the Internet. *From the Westlaw Web site, www.westlaw.com. Used with the permission of West Group.*

Regardless of which interface you use—the Internet or dial-up—research strategies are the same. This introductory chapter orients you to using our research strategies with Westlaw. Later chapters focus on additional searching skills using Westlaw. Before doing the exercises in this chapter, you should have a basic familiarity with Westlaw.[3]

Westlaw uses a number of Boolean search features:

- **Boolean operators.** Westlaw uses the Boolean search operators AND, OR, BUT, NOT, and /n. The default search operator is OR.

- **Proximity search.** There are several options for proximity searching. In addition to the /n operator, you can look for terms in the same sentence (/s, +s) and in the same paragraph (/p, +p).

- **Phrase search.** Westlaw permits phrase searching with quotation marks. For example, you can search for the phrase "unauthorized practice of law." Of course, the search ignores the word *of*, as it is a stopword.

- **Stemming.** Westlaw automatically activates the stemming feature, retrieving plurals and possessives of the search terms.

- **Wildcard.** To perform a wildcard search in Westlaw, use the asterisk (*). For example, *wom*n* retrieves the words *women, woman,* and *womyn.* To find all variations of a word, use an exclamation point (!) at the end of a word.

Westlaw's support materials and Help page have more information on its search features.

Lexis

Figure 3-3: Lexis logo. *From the Lexis-Nexis Web site, www.lexis-nexis.com.*

Lexis-Nexis is another of the original providers of electronic legal research. It provides access to a broad array of information. The Lexis side provides primary and secondary sources of law including legal journals, hornbooks, and legal periodicals. It provides bill tracking tools (for law that has not yet been created) and legislative history tools (for exploring the background of law as it was being created). The Nexis side provides non-legal news and information, including access to hundreds of newspapers, trade journals, newsletters, and other information sources.

In the past, researchers accessed Lexis through a dial-up connection. In a dial-up connection, the researchers computer "dials up" or calls the Lexis computer. A researcher had to install Lexis software on her computer and was then generally restricted to searching from that computer or another with Lexis software installed. Today more and more Lexis subscribers access its services through the Internet at Lexis.com (**www.lexis.com**), so they can use the Lexis-Nexis databases while working on any computer with an Internet connection. No special Lexis software is needed to access its database over the Internet.

Figure 3-4: Lexis.com. You can access the Lexis libraries over the Internet. *From the Lexis Web site, www.lexis.com.*

Regardless of which interface you use—the Internet or dial-up—research strategies are the same. This chapter introduces you to using research strategies in Lexis. Later chapters teach you additional searching skills. Before doing the exercises in this chapter, you should have a basic understanding of Lexis.

When you try to find information electronically, visualizing its organization is important. Without this understanding, you will have difficulty finding the documents you want. One way to visualize the organization of Lexis is knowing that the information is in separate libraries. Imagine that each library has different floors and that each room on each floor contains certain information.

Lexis uses the following Boolean search features:

- **Boolean operators.** Lexis uses the Boolean search operators AND, OR, NOT, /n, and NOT /n.

- **Proximity search.** In addition to the /n operator, several options are available for proximity searching. You can look for terms in the same sentence (/s) and in the same paragraph (/p).

- **Phrase search.** Lexis permits phrase searching with quotation marks. For example, you can search for the phrase "unauthorized practice of law." Of course, the search ignores the word *of*, as it is a stopword.

- **Stemming.** Lexis automatically activates the stemming feature to retrieve plurals and possessives. Lexis also automatically retrieves word equivalents. For example, a search for *wash.* returns the words *WA* and *Washington*.

- **Wildcard.** You can perform a wildcard search in Lexis by using the asterisk (*). For example, a search for *wom*n* retrieves the words *women*, *woman*, and *womyn*. Placed at the end of a word, an exclamation point brings back all variations of that word.

For more information on Boolean search features, see the Lexis support materials and Help sections.

Exercise 3-1
> Practice using the Boolean search operators with Lexis and Westlaw by answering the questions in Exercise 3-1 at the end of this chapter.

Other Paid Legal Databases

Lexis and Westlaw are definitely the major players when it comes to comprehensive legal databases. Their services are like those available at the largest university law libraries, which offer everything, including the most obscure law review or treatise. However, space, cost, and convenience also create the need for smaller law libraries—libraries that house information on local statutes and case law, local law reviews, popular practice books, and treatises. Not surprisingly, electronic services have evolved to fill that niche in the electronic legal research world as well. Dozens of companies provide reliable, basic state and federal information for a fraction of the cost of the Lexis and Westlaw services. To many attorneys who have focused practices and need only limited research materials, these types of services are especially attractive.

Since dozens of providers offer different local information, addressing them all in this text is impossible. Fortunately, we do not need to. Chapter 1 discussed how all electronic research is basically the same; if you understand how to use one legal database, you can quickly and easily figure out how to use another. Keep that in mind as you read about two representative small legal databases—CD Law and Loislaw. Each has features that differ from Lexis and Westlaw. The following sections give you a general idea of how to use smaller legal databases.

Loislaw

Figure 3-5: Loislaw logo. *From the Loislaw Web site, www.loislaw.com. Used with the permission of Loislaw, a Division of Aspen Publishers, Inc.*

The Loislaw legal database is accessible only over the Internet. It has a national scope and contains case law, statutory law, constitutions, administrative law, court rules, and other authority for all fifty states, the District of Columbia, and the decisions of the federal Supreme Court and Court of Appeals. In general, Loislaw does not include secondary sources like law journals or encyclopedia.

Small firms and sole practitioners find small databases like Loislaw useful because they are far less expensive than Westlaw and Lexis. In addition, sometimes finding what you are looking for in a smaller database is easier because there is less to search through.

Although searching Loislaw slightly differs from searching other resources this chapter has explored, it is the same at its core. Here is a list of some notable features.

- **Boolean operators.** Loislaw uses the Boolean operators AND, OR, NOT, and NEAR. It also allows the use of symbols for searching. For example, the ampersand (&) symbol represents AND, and a vertical line (|) represents OR, default operator. The Loislaw Help section explains all the symbols for the connectors.

- **Proximity search.** Proximity searching is possible using NEAR and specifying the number of words for the proximity search. For example, if you are looking for *battery* within five words of *child*, you would enter *battery NEAR5 child*. If you are doing multiple proximities, use parentheses to help. For example, if you want to find *battery* within five words of *child* and *battery* within five words of *abuse*, you might try this query: *battery NEAR5 (child OR abuse)*. Insiders at Loislaw say that the NEAR operator is their favorite for searching their databases.

- **Phrase search.** You do a phrase search in Loislaw by using quotation marks. For example, you can search for the phrase *"unauthorized practice of law."* Of course, the search ignores the word *of*, as it is a stopword.

- **Stemming.** Loislaw automatically looks for the most common variations of single words. For example, if you search for the word *child*, Loislaw also looks for *children, childish*, and *childlike*.

- **Wildcard.** The question mark (?) is a wildcard for single characters within a word or number. For example, a search for *wom?n* finds *women, woman* and *womyn*. Using the asterisk guides Loislaw to search for all variations of a word or number. For example, if you are uncertain of a date, searching for *199** finds documents created any time during the nineties. Use the asterisk only at the end of a word or number.

Loislaw's support materials and Help page offer more information on searching.

CD Law

Figure 3-6: CD Law logo. *From the CD Law Web site, www.cdlaw.com.*

CD-ROM
portable disk that can store large quantities of electronic data.

CD Law started, as you can imagine from its name, as a **CD-ROM** subscription service, one of the nation's first. One of many single state databases, CD Law focuses entirely on the law of Washington State. With such a narrow focus, single state databases like CD Law can include hard-to-obtain collections that larger services miss, including local domestic forms, local hearings board decisions, and county codes. They may also contain some federal law like the United States Code and the Federal Rules of Civil Procedure.

Every month, CD Law sends subscribers new CDs updating the law and keeping subscribers current. The CD-ROM format lets researchers take their time because they do not need to worry about the high per minute charges typical of Lexis and Westlaw. Now, like other services, CD Law has moved to the Web, where court decisions are updated daily. Even with the entire database available online, many still prefer doing research with the CD-ROM, which continues to be the basis of the CD Law service.

While CD Law is dedicated to Washington State law, similar CD-ROM services exist throughout the country. A review of CD Law is useful in understanding those services as well.

The CD-ROM isn't Dead

Discussion with Scott Wetzel, President of CD Law. With the world turning so rapidly to the Internet as the preferred tool for legal research, what is the future for CD-ROM products? "The CD-ROM isn't dead," said CD Law's Scott Wetzel. Indeed, recent market studies show that many legal practitioners prefer the CD-ROM format. Rather than abandon CD-ROM, Wetzel affirms that CD Law has "its feet planted firmly in both worlds." CD Law has an easy-to-use Web site (www.cdlaw.com) where subscribers can access all its databases. It also adopted a hybrid model for presenting information, including links to the Internet in its CD-ROM products. Through an association with Lexis, CD Law subscribers can click on a Shepardize button from the CD-ROM to start the Web browser and see Shepard's results in Lexis.com. This type of innovation keeps CD Law at the forefront of local legal research.

Searching CD Law is straightforward, as it uses Boolean search operators. In addition, CD Law provides a **Table of Contents** feature and case-to-statute cross-referencing via internal hypertext links. This means you can click on a link to the statutory reference within a case to open that section of the statute in another window for easy research.

The Table of Contents feature is especially useful. Similar to browsing through books, the feature sets out the table of contents of the state and federal codes. This helps in two ways. First, if you have a partial citation or you have difficulty forming a query to find that document, you can use the Table of Contents feature to go directly to the section you are looking for. (CD Law does not have a citation search like Westlaw and Lexis.) Second, if you are unsure what you want, or you know but cannot think of the right keywords, the Table of Contents feature lets you find the information by stepping through the law one section at a time.

Here is a summary of CD Law's Boolean search features.

Table of Contents
like a book's table of contents, this feature lets you see what sections of the law are available and easily access those sections.

- **Boolean operators.** CD Law uses the Boolean search operators AND, OR, NOT, NEAR, **ADJ** (meaning *adjacent to*, similar to a proximity search operator), and /n. The default search operator is ADJ.

- **Proximity search.** The default search ADJ automatically leads to proximity searching.

- **Phrase search.** CD Law permits phrase searching with single quotation marks. For example, you can search for the phrase "unauthorized practice of law." Of course, the search ignores the stopword *of*.

ADJ (adjacent to)
Boolean search operator that requires the search terms be adjacent to or next to each other. It is very similar to the phrase operator, but with ADJ, terms can appear in any order.

- **Stemming.** CD Law automatically activates the stemming feature that permits you to search for the most common varieties of a single word. For example, a search for the word *child* also finds the words *children*, *childish*, and *childlike*.

- **Wildcard.** You can perform a wildcard search in CD Law by using the question mark (?). For example, a search for *wom?n* finds the words *women*, *woman*, and *womyn*. A question mark at the end of a word finds all variations of that word.

CD law's support materials and Help page offer more information on its search features.

Exercise 3-2

Practice using a small paid legal database by doing Exercise 3-2 at the end of this chapter.

Beginning Your Research

In Chapter 2, we looked at Five Questions, a systematic way to begin a research project:

Question 1: What is the general legal topic?
Question 2: What type of law am I looking for?
Question 3: What secondary sources do I investigate?
Question 4: Where can I look for relevant information?
Question 5: How do I formulate my query?

Let's use the Five Questions and your favorite paid legal database to explore the following scenario:

> *Shannon Proctor rents a small, one-bedroom apartment for twelve months. When she moves in, she pays a $1000 refundable deposit. She has no written agreement with the landlord. Shannon then decides to buy a condo and finds a perfect one not far away. When the closing date is determined, Shannon writes a letter to give her landlord 30-days notice. Furious at Shannon's short notice, the landlord refuses to return her deposit, despite the immaculate condition of the apartment. Shannon wants to sue to get her deposit back. Can she prevail?*

Question 1: What is the general legal topic?

Here, the general legal topic is *landlord tenant* law under the broader category of *real property*. Knowing these general topics helps you to focus your research.

Question 2: What type of law am I looking for?

Most states have a Landlord Tenant Act, which is *state statutory* law. In addition, there may be some cases on the subject. The cases are also likely to fall under state law.

Question 3: What secondary sources do I investigate?

If we keep focusing on state law, it might include some *state law review articles* that explain landlord-tenant law. Does your state have a *landlord tenant practice book* for local attorneys? Such a resource may be available electronically via specialized databases. If not, do not be afraid to use any available printed resources. (The electronic researcher often forgets that books are still very useful.) Another resource might be the Web site of tenant rights advocates. It is easy to overlook Web sites; they are useful secondary sources in their own right.

Question 3 is easier to answer if you know something about the subject. If you have difficulty finding specific secondary sources, do not be afraid to stick with the basics—a legal dictionary and a legal encyclopedia.

Question 4: Where can I look for relevant information?

To answer this question, focus on a specific section of your paid legal database. Where exactly do you expect to find the answer? To find the actual Landlord Tenant Act, you should explore the statute section of your specific state.

For secondary sources, stick with the state section, this time exploring the secondary source area. What relevant secondary sources are available in your state directory?

Question 5: How do I formulate my query?

To answer this question, you need to determine keywords. Sometimes crafting an issue statement can help you determine the keywords. Here, a good issue statement might be:

> *Whether a tenant can get her deposit back when she gave her landlord a 30-day notice and the parties had no other written agreement?*

Within this issue statement are some keywords for this topic: tenant, deposit, notice. Why these keywords? First, although the topic is landlord tenant law, you rarely find a document that talks about tenants without referring to or being relevant to landlords. So, there is no need to use both words; just tenant (or landlord) works fine. Deposit is the focus of our issue question—can Shannon get her deposit back? Finally, notice is important because the landlord alleges insufficient notice is the reason for retaining the deposit. While you might be tempted to add written agreement, the phrase might eliminate some useful documents. Save it for a focus search.

Once you identify keywords, you are ready to put them together in a way that brings back the information you need. Formulating the query is the focus of the following guided exercises.

Guided Exercises

This guided exercise is designed to help you systematically explore how your favorite paid legal database works and how to find information there. Be patient and take notes. If you have a printed instruction manual for the paid legal database, write your notes right in the manual as you work through the exercise. That way, the notes are easily available to you later. If you have no manual, print the most relevant sections of the online Help manual, and use your printed pages as a handy reference.

Before you begin the guided exercise, take note of the following:

- Most paid legal databases do not let you query until you select a specific database to search. Deciding on the appropriate database is part of the answer to Question 4 of the Five Questions.

terms and connectors used in Lexis to indicate Boolean search operators.

- Our lessons focus on Boolean or **terms and connectors** searching. Initially, Boolean searching can be more difficult than the natural language searching that both Lexis and Westlaw permit, but once you master it, terms and connectors searching yields much more specific results. When your employer pays by the minute to use Lexis and Westlaw, the accuracy of your results becomes very important. Also, skills you learn doing Boolean searching on paid legal databases directly apply to your searching the Internet and other databases. For those reasons, focus on Boolean searching in this exercise and throughout the exercises in the text.

By far, the easiest thing to do in paid legal databases is getting a document when you have an exact citation. However, it is in performing this simple task that some of the more frustrating mistakes occur.

1. **Go to your paid legal database.** Select a database for finding the landmark case *Miranda v Arizona*, 384 US 436 (1966). Remember to select the source most narrowly designed to meet your needs. For example, the United States Supreme Court is a federal body, so the database you select should include only federal, not state, resources. Selecting a database narrowly suited to your needs limits the number of search results because you are searching fewer documents. Having fewer, more targeted results makes finding what you are looking for easier.

2. **Select a specific file in that database.** Remember to go narrow. Do not try to rush through the selection process. Read your options carefully. When you are more familiar with the options, you can select more quickly.

3. **Form a query.** The purpose of the query is to find the case *Miranda v Arizona*, 384 US 436 (1966). As you create your query, remember that all terms must have a connector. For example, if you want a case on the elements of battery, do not enter

      Elements battery

Rather, you might enter

      Elements AND battery or

      Elements /s battery

Note the connector between all terms. If you do not use a connector, the database automatically uses the default operator. Also note that you must place connectors between terms and you must not begin or end a query with a connector. What query did you enter for *Miranda v Arizona*? How many hits did you get? Evaluate your results—did you get what you wanted?[4]

4. **Find the same case using the citation-specific search tool in your paid legal database.** In Lexis, this specific tool is called Lexsee,[5] in Westlaw it is Find. Loislaw's Advanced Search section permits a citation search.[6] Now how many hits did you get?

When searching for a single document with a citation in the future, which method would you use and why?

Now let's try a more complicated activity—searching to find the answer to a scenario.

Your clients, Mr. and Mrs. Douglas, have a precocious eight-year-old son named Ricky. Last week, Ricky ventured into old Mr. Hanson's backyard (which closely resembles a junkyard) ignoring the no trespassing signs. Ricky had to climb a fence and bribe Mr. Hanson's dog with a bone to get to his goal—an old, rusty convertible. While playing in the old car, Ricky fell and broke his wrist. His parents want to sue Mr. Hanson for having such a dangerous yard in a neighborhood with several children. Mr. Hanson says he put up several barriers to entry and if the child ignored them and was injured, it was the child's fault. Do Mr. and Mrs. Douglas have a case?

Answer the Five Questions for this fact scenario.

Question 1: What is the general legal topic?
Question 2: What kind of law am I looking for?
Question 3: What secondary sources do I investigate?
Question 4: Where can I look for relevant information? In other words, in what specific directory of my paid legal database will I look to find the information?
Question 5: How do I formulate my query? What keywords do I use? Refer to the hints below for help. Don't forget to use the hints that you learned in the previous section. See the end of the chapter for hints in answering this guided exercise.[7]

- **Keyword Hint:** Remember that several words may be appropriate. Here, you may wish to use the word *injured* or *injury*. (Do not use the phrase *broken bones* or *broken wrist*—that is too specific.) You can use the OR connector or a wildcard operator like * or !. (The term *injur!* finds both *injured* and *injury*.)

- **Proximity Search Hint:** When searching for a fairly general term like *injury*, it is helpful to narrow the term by using other relevant keywords. However, you may also find that having your keywords close together is helpful. Using AND finds the keywords in the same document, but they might be completely unrelated, leading to lots of useless results. Suppose your keywords are *injury* and *child*. You might want to find *injury* and *child* in the same paragraph (/p) or in the same sentence (/s). One of this author's favorite connectors, however, is the number search (/n, where a number like 5 or 10 replaces the n). The number search works best with smaller numbers. If n is more than 10 or 15, you might as well use the sentence or paragraph proximity searches; both are very effective as well.

SUMMARY

As you learned while doing the exercises, there are more similarities than differences between the paid legal databases. All use Boolean search operators as the basic method of retrieving documents from their vast databases. The comparison table at the end of the chapter shows just how similar the databases are.

In addition to looking at technical aspects of searching different databases, we looked at how to use a search strategy like the Five Questions to do research in the paid legal databases. If you continue to practice applying a search strategy when you research, you will find it becomes second nature and significantly speeds your research.

Notes

1. You can find links to the tutorials on the Web site that supports this text.
2. *Discovering Westlaw*, 9th ed.
3. For Westlaw orientation links, see the Web site that supports this text.
4. When you do a typical query for a citation or party names, the database finds not only the document you requested, but every document that cites that document. For a case as famous as Miranda, that means a lot of documents. If available, use the hyperlinked reference to your case to find the actual text quickly.
5. Lexsee is for caselaw: Lexstat does the same for statutes.
6. CD Law does not have federal cases.
7. Answers to the questions: What is your issue question? *Is it a battery when one car strikes another?*
   What is the general topic of law involved? *Intentional torts, criminal law*
   What kind of law are you looking for? *Case law for tort, statutory for criminal*
   Would it be state or federal? *state*
   In what Lexis library and file will you find the information? *States Legal– Washington–Washington Cases, admin and AG opinions*
   What key words will you use? *Car, vehicle, automobile*

EXERCISES

Exercise 3-1

Form a query from the following issue statements using the connectors of your favorite paid legal database.

1. Whether nonprofit organizations can sue when a donor fails to give a promised gift

2. Whether an environmental group can buy timber harvest rights when it has no intention of cutting wood

3. Whether a person who shares information with a bank for a loan has a right of privacy over personal information

4. Whether a nurse would lose her license if she took patient medication for personal use

5. Whether a college is liable for cleanup costs when an alum donates a piece of contaminated property

Exercise 3-2

Review statements 1 through 5 in Exercise 3-1. How would the queries differ if you used your favorite smaller electronic database?

Chapter Review Exercises

In Chapter 2, you prepared the Five Questions for the following fact scenarios. Now, do the actual research and answer the questions.

1. Greg and Erich entered into an agreement for Erich to buy a classic guitar from Greg for $950. They had no written agreement; the men just shook hands. Greg told Erich that the guitar would be ready in one week. When Erich arrived at the appointed time to get the guitar, Greg decided he did not want to sell. Erich wants to enforce the agreement. Can he?

2. Dastardly Doug decided to rob the home of Sally Sloppy. While in the house, Doug fell on a bicycle in the hall and sprained his ankle. Doug wants to sue Sally for negligence. Can he prevail?

3. Click and Clack buy an old beach house as joint tenants. For many years, the brothers enjoyed the house together. When Click prepared his will, he left his part of the home to his son Clunk. Is his bequest valid?

4. After recovering from the sprained ankle, Dastardly Doug decided to rob a jewelry store. Doug wore a black ski mask but was unarmed. When Doug entered the store, old Mr. Diamond was so horrified that he had a heart attack and died. Can Doug be charged for murder?

5. Ken recently started having stomach problems. He thinks that during surgery five years ago, his doctor left a sponge in his tummy. He wonders if it is too late to sue the doctor for malpractice. Is it?

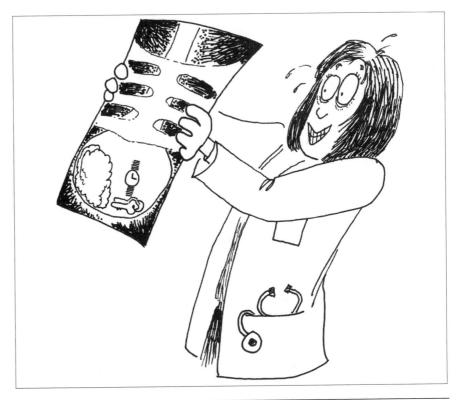

Figure 3-7: "Hey! There's that sponge…and my watch…are those my keys?!?"
Illustration by Joe Mills. Reprinted with permission. All rights reserved.

Paid Legal Database Comparison Table				
Database	*Boolean (default in boldface)*	*Proximity Search*	*Phrase Search*	*Stemming*	*Wildcard*
Westlaw	AND, **OR**, BUT NOT, /n	/s, +s /p, +p	"Quotation marks"	Automatic	* single letter ! at end of word
Lexis	AND, **OR**, NOT, /n, NOT /n	/s /p	"Quotation marks"	Automatic	* single letter ! at end of word
Loislaw	AND, **OR**, NOT, NEAR	NEAR#	"Quotation marks"	Automatic	? single letter * at end of word
CD Law	AND, OR, NOT, NEAR, **ADJ**	ADJ	Single 'quotation mark'	Automatic	? for single letter or at end of word

Worksheet

New Database Worksheet

Use this worksheet to determine relevant search information when finding databases.

Database:

_____

Boolean:

_____

Proximity Search:

_____

Phrase Search:

_____

Stemming:

_____

Wildcard:

Worksheet

Paid Legal Database Research Toolbox

Use this worksheet to comment on the Web sites featured in this chapter and to include information on your own favorites.

Website: Westlaw (**www.westlaw.com**)

Favorite Features:

Comments:

Website: Lexis (**www.lexis.com**)

Favorite Features:

Comments:

Web site: Loislaw (**www.loislaw.com**)

Favorite Features:

Comments:

Web site: CD Law (**www.cdlaw.com**)

Favorite Features:

Comments:

4

Internet Legal Research

Chapter Objectives

- **Where to search for information:** Different search engines perform different tasks. Learn the difference between a search engine, a directory and a meta search tool.

- **How to search for information:** Apply your developing Boolean search skills to Internet databases.

- **How to check information credibility:** Anyone can put a site on the Internet, so looking into the validity of information is important.

- **Build your Internet toolbox:** Create your own list of favorite research sites using a set of logical criteria.

On the Web:

- Annotated links leading you to:
  - History of the Internet
  - Using the Internet—a guide to resources
  - Evaluating search engines
  - Evaluating the credibility of Web sites
  - Sites mentioned in this chapter

- Exercises for additional help

Welcome to the Internet

Internet

also known as the Net. A collection of linked computers that lets users review and exchange information. The Internet includes features like e-mail, telnet, bulletin boards, instant messaging, and the World Wide Web.

World Wide Web

also known as WWW or the Web. A collection of computers that allows users to access information through an appealing graphical interface. It lets Web sites have images, colors, and other interesting features, rather than just plain text.

The **Internet** is basically a collection of computers linked together. With the proper tools, you can call from one computer to other computers and get information from them. One part of the Internet is the World Wide Web, a collection of graphical interfaces that makes moving between pages and Web sites simple. The creation of the **World Wide Web** (WWW) lowered the technical wall that separated techies from non-techies, making it easy for the most inexperienced person to enjoy the benefits of the Internet. The World Wide Web is also a great resource for the legal researcher, as it lets you do things that most people could not even imagine just a few years ago. For example, from your home computer you can now do research that would have required you to spend time at a major law library ten years ago. You can also access resources that you may not readily find in a law library—brief banks, forms, and so on. However, despite the hype, the Internet will not replace the law library or paid legal databases any time soon. For the most part, legal collections on the Internet are limited and require more skill and patience to access than paid legal databases. For that reason, the Internet is only one of many tools you use for legal research.

When doing any kind of research on the Internet, you need to know three things:

1. Where to look
2. How to look
3. How to determine the validity of what you find

This chapter discusses each of those topics.

Where to Look for Information

Search engine

tool that lets you search through information on the Internet.

Internet Service Provider

also known as an ISP. The company that gives you access to the Internet, your on-ramp to the information superhighway. ISP facilitates your ability to dial up the Internet through a modem or have constant access to the Internet fast Internet connections.

The average person who looks for information on the Internet generally does a search on the **search engine** that first appears on the computer screen. Depending on the **Internet service provider** (ISP) used, the search engine may be Netscape Netcenter, MSN.com, AOL, Netfind or one of many others. More advanced users might head to a popular "search engine" like Yahoo! or Alta Vista. Most people do not know that not all search engines are alike. Indeed, the difference is the results you get from your search can be huge, depending on which search tool you use and how you use it.

What is a Search Engine?

A search engine is a tool used to search the Internet. It is very similar to the search boxes used in paid legal databases. Used generically, the term *search engine* includes all kinds of search tools. These tools generally fit into one of five categories:

- search engines
- search directories
- hybrid search engines

- meta search tools
- specialty search tools

The next sections examine each of the tools.

Search Engines

A search engine searches the Web using continuously running computer indexing programs known as crawlers or spiders. The spiders constantly scurry around the World Wide Web searching for new Web pages. They report their findings to the search engine. Search engine indexes are created automatically, and they contain the sites that the spiders find. So, when you perform a search, you do not search the entire Web. Rather, you search the index created by the spiders. Many search engines advertise the size of their index. In general, the larger the index, the better the opportunity for great results.

Since the index is created automatically, humans might or might not sort through the sites that the spiders find. As a result, your search might yield thousands of hits and hundreds of them will be irrelevant or repetitive. Suppose you search for the word *tort* trying to find its definition. Depending where you look, you could get many more results than you want because your search might find every mention of *tort*—whether it refers to a legal action or a dessert. Indeed, on one search engine, a query for the word *tort* resulted in 58,042 hits, most completely irrelevant.

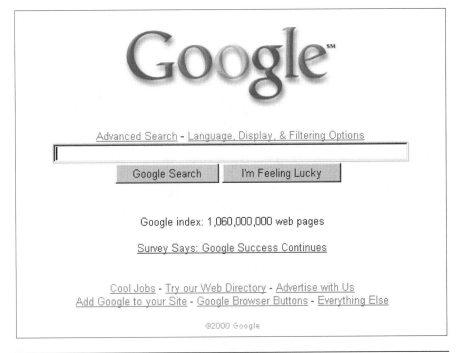

Figure 4-1: Google claims to have the Web's largest index. Professional researchers hail Google as the best search engine on the Web. *From www.google.com. Used with the permission of Google Inc. All rights reserved. Google is a trademark of Google Inc.*

Some of the top-ranked search engines are Google (**www.google.com**), Alta Vista (**www.altavista.com**), Northern Light (**www.northernlight.com**), and Excite (**www.excite.com**).

When you enter a search query, you probably assume you are getting the most relevant information that the index has to offer. However, more and more Web site owners are willing to pay for the privilege of appearing high on your results list. If you run a search and get 58,000 hits, chances are you will only look at the first ten to twenty sites listed. Web sites know this and are willing to pay to be among the top hits on your list. Indeed, some search engines charge Web sites to even be included in their indexes. The major search directory Yahoo! is among those that charge businesses to be included in its index. Check the URL submission page of a search engine to see if it charges Web sites to appear in the results list. You can generally find this information at the bottom of the search engine's home page as a link with a title like "submit a site."

Search Directories

Search directory
search tool that breaks sites into categories to facilitate browsing.

Search spiders also hunt down Web sites for **search directories**, but humans review the results and sort them into categories like Government, Entertainment, and Travel. When you search a search directory, you do not search the entire Web or even a large index of it. Rather, you search the smaller number of categorized sites in the directory. This results in fewer, but frequently more relevant, hits. On the other hand, if you search for something rather obscure or something that does not fall into one of the categories, you may get no hits at all.

Browsing
looking through ordered lists of information, generally arranged hierarchically, to find information you want. One might browse a table of contents or a subject area of directory.

Search directories also facilitate **browsing**. If you are not entirely sure what you are looking for, a directory makes it easy to start with a broad concept— like law—and work your way to a very specific concept—like sentencing.

Some top-ranked search directories include Yahoo! (**www.yahoo.com**) and Web Crawler (**www.webcrawler.com**).

This chapter includes the top-ranked search tools. Quite a few organizations rank search tools[1] using a variety of criteria, but the most popular criteria include:

♦ relevancy of links
♦ absence of duplicate or broken links
♦ speed of results
♦ number of pages indexed

Hybrid Search Tools

Hybrid search tool
search tool that contains both a search engine and a search directory.

So, you cannot figure out whether to search or browse? You can get the best of both worlds by using a **hybrid search tool** that combines the search engine with the search directory. This approach is becoming more and more popular, and many search engines are adding directories to make searching the Web easier. Sites included in the directory are frequently the most popular sites and often have reviews written by the search engine staff. Sites like Alta Vista (**www.altavista.com**) and Infoseek (**www.infoseek.com**) jumped on the directory bandwagon, giving you the convenience of Web and directory searching under one roof.

Meta Search Tools

With so many great search tools on the Web, deciding which to use can be very hard. But why choose? The **meta search tool** makes life simple by taking your query and submitting it to several search tools simultaneously. Metacrawler (**www.metacrawler.com**), one of the oldest and best Web search tools, simultaneously searches seven or eight popular search tools and brings back only the most relevant hits, frequently fewer than thirty or forty. Dogpile (**www.dogpile.com**) and Ask Jeeves (**www.ask.com**) are also popular meta search tools.

Meta search tools
search engines that
search several search
engines at once.

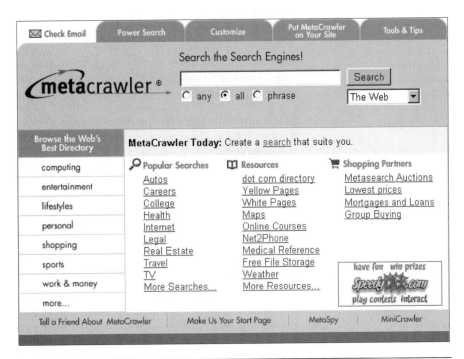

Figure 4-2: Metacrawler was one of the original meta search engines. Like other search engines, it now hosts a Web directory and other services. *From www.metacrawler.com.*

Specialty Search Tools

Sometimes searching a large index of the World Wide Web for specific information is a bit too much. For specialty searches like legal or medical issues, you wish someone would just find all law- or medicine-related sites and then let you

Specialty search tools
search engines and
directories dedicated to
specific topics like law or
medicine.

search through them. Fortunately, **specialty search tools** grant your wish. One of the best specialty search engines for law is the combination of LawCrawler (a legal search engine) and FindLaw (a legal search directory). You can access both at **www.findlaw.com**.

How to Look for Information

Looking for information on the Internet is very similar to looking for information in paid legal databases. As discussed in Chapter 1, electronic research is basically the same, regardless of the information source. Because of that, you can effectively search the Internet using the Boolean operators and search strategies described in earlier chapters. In addition to traditional Boolean search operators, several search tools use modified Boolean searching or their own search terms. Here's a look at some very common alternative search techniques you will encounter on the Internet.

- **Plus (+) and Minus (–):** Some search engines opt for simpler versions of Boolean operators with the + and – symbols. The + symbol indicates that you want to include a term, and the – symbol means you want to exclude a term. The method is similar to using AND and NOT in Boolean searching. When using the plus and minus symbols, remember to place them directly in front of the word, with no space, for example, **+battery –car**.

- **Title operator (t:):** Use the letter *t* followed by a colon and the keyword to search for that keyword in the title of a document. Add no spaces between the *t*, the colon, and the keyword, for example, **t:battery**.

- **URL operator (u:):** A **URL** (Universal Resource Locator) is a Web site address. For example, **www.panamacanal.com** is the URL for a Panama Canal touring company. Use the letter *u* followed by a colon and a keyword to search for the keyword in a URL, for example, **u:battery**.[2]

Search Strategies

The average person who goes to the Web to find information generally "searches" for that information. To search, the person goes to a favorite search engine, types a term, and hopes for the best. This strategy works well in about one-quarter of search situations. In other situations, you—as a skilled Internet researcher—must use some thoughtful strategies for finding information on the Web.

Searching vs. Browsing

Imagine a trip to the mall. Let's say you need a new pair of jeans. You target the stores most likely to have jeans. When you enter the store, you go right to the jeans section to look for what you want. If you do not find it, you go to another store. This is the equivalent of searching.

Now suppose you just feel like shopping for clothes, but you do not specifically need jeans. You may be inclined to wander around the store and then stop and look more closely at whatever captures your interest. This is the equivalent of browsing.

Thus, searching and browsing are similar to shopping for jeans. How does this translate into legal terms? Imagine you are looking for information on the contract remedy of *specific performance*. If you were to do what most people do, you would go to a general search engine, type the phrase *specific performance*, and hope for the best. Your results might include *specific* art *performances* or the *performance* of *specific* ships in an armada. Unfortunately, that is not exactly what you were looking for. Since you have a specific search need, you should utilize a more specific tool. Go to a legal site, preferably one dedicated to information about contracts, and look for exactly what you want. Why search the entire Web when you can find what you need in a specific place that you know? Doing so is like going to every store in the mall looking for jeans when only some stores sell clothes.

On the browsing side, if you only vaguely know what you want, broad searches are far more appropriate: The wide variety of results may give you some good ideas. When you know you are browsing, use a search directory like Yahoo! or FindLaw. In this case, if you go to FindLaw, then go to legal subjects, then to contracts, you can browse sites to explore remedy options, eventually finding that Specific Performance meets your needs.

Exercise 4-1

Practice searching and browsing by answering the questions in Exercise 4-1 at the end of the chapter.

Guessing the URL

People often feel that searching is the only way to find information on the Web. Actually, if you basically know where you are going, performing a traditional search may be the slowest way to get there. Do you take time to look up your best friend's phone number when you have it memorized? Probably not. By the same token, for many sites, if you know the company or organization name, you know its Web site address. Look at these examples:

- Delmar Publishers (**www.delmar.com**)

- American Heart Association (**www.americanheart.org**)

- Environmental Protection Agency (**www.epa.gov**)

The tricky thing to remember is the kind of place you are trying to access. Is it a company or business that sells things? If so, chances are its URL has the *.com* suffix. Is it a government agency? Expect the *.gov* suffix. How about a club, group, or other nonprofit organization? Expect to see the *.org* suffix at the end of its name. Finally, if you are looking for a college, university, grade school, or other educational institution, tack *.edu* on the end.

Hints for Guessing the Web Site Name

- If the name is long, try using an abbreviation like NYU for New York University (**www.nyu.edu**).

- International organizations often add *America*, *USA*, or *US* to their Web site names, for example, Toyota USA (**www.toyotaUSA.com**) or the United States Supreme Court (**www.supremecourtus.gov**).

- Remember that a Web site address contains no spaces. For example, the Sierra Club is **www.sierraclub.org**.

So, you can see how simple guessing a Web site address is. When you know where you are going, it is really useful to know that guessing may be a better use of your time than traditional searching.

How to Determine the Credibility of What You Find

The Internet is a mountain of information. Your first challenge is to find what you are looking for. Your second challenge is to determine whether what you found is trustworthy. Anyone can create a Web site and post on it any information they choose. Not all the information is true or credible. This is true of any media. However, on the Internet and on the sites you visit, you must be especially vigilant in determining the validity of information.

Fortunately, making an initial determination of a site's credibility is fairly easy. You can do it by asking two key questions: What is the purpose of this site? How current is the information?

What is the Purpose of This Site?

When looking for credible information on the Internet, being aware of why the information is there is really important. Is it there to educate? Are the site sponsors trying to sell you something? Are they trying to persuade you to take a certain viewpoint? One way to determine a site's purpose is to think about who placed the site on the Internet. Generally, Web site sponsors belong to one of four groups: educational or governmental organizations, businesses, nonprofit organizations, and individuals.

Educational Institutions or Government Organizations

These sites are usually a safe bet for credible information, but you should still be alert. Generally, their purpose is to educate the visitor. One thing to watch for are student Web sites. With an *.edu* extension, student Web sites look like school-sponsored sites. However, most schools that let students create personal Web sites are not involved in those sites' content. Consider them in the same manner as you consider individuals' sites.

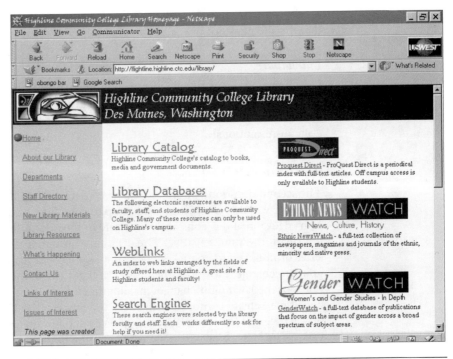

Figure 4-3: Highline Library. Information provided by educational institutions is generally very useful. *From http://flightline.highline.ctc.edu/library.*

Businesses

Generally, these sites have a financial motive for providing information. Businesses want to educate you or tempt you to buy their products. That does not mean that the information is not credible, but it does mean that you should look at the information critically. Check the validity of the information by seeing if you can find similar information on other sites.

Law Firm Web Sites

More and more law firms are on the net providing useful information. Do not be less vigilant because the information comes from a lawyer. Law firms are businesses too.

Nonprofit organizations

These organizations generally have biases that you should be aware of. Indeed, all information is biased in some manner, so thinking critically about information that you encounter helps to heighten your awareness of information that is biased. However, just because an organization presents information for a biased reason does not mean that the information is not useful. It may mean, however, that the site does not present you with both sides of an issue.

Individuals

If information seems to come from an individual, examine the person's credentials and make sure the person has the background to present information authoritatively. If no credential information is available, treat the information even more cautiously.

How Current Is the Information?

The second question you should ask when determining the credibility of information is whether the information is up to date. Law changes with every new court decision and is constantly in a state of flux. Because of that, much legal information is time sensitive. The decision of whether information is time sensitive or not is yours to make. For example, a legal decision made in 1984 is not going to change. However, the impact of that case on the law and the current status of the law might change, making that information time sensitive. If you need time-sensitive information, check to see when the Web site was last updated. Some sites are placed on the Web and not updated for months or even years. The "Last Updated" date is often at the bottom of a page in small print. If that information is not available, you should be especially cautious with time-sensitive information.

Your Internet Toolbox

The Internet is full of lists of links telling you the *best* places to find information. But what determines whether a site is the *best*? Different people would answer the question differently. For the businessperson, the best site might be the one that gets the most hits. For the Web developer, it might be the site with the best design. For you, as a legal researcher, the answer will depend on what you are looking for. However, the researcher should look for a few basic criteria that fall under two categories: information and technology.

A heightened awareness of information and technology issues can help you evaluate which sites are better than others. As an effective legal researcher, it is important that your research information come from only the most credible and reliable sources, preferably those that are well organized and maintained. Remember, your client depends on it.

As a legal researcher, your collection of favorite sites will be what facilitates your effective legal research. You should never be completely satisfied with your list; regularly search the Web for new and better sites to add to your list, and discard sites that no longer serve your needs. Throughout the coming chapters, you will build a site collection that will be the foundation of your effective Internet researching for years to come.

Information

Here are some tips for evaluating information.

- Is the information on the site trustworthy? Did the site pass the credibility questions with flying colors? If not, you should probably not include it in your legal research favorites—although you may enjoy the site for other purposes.

- Is the information easy to find? It does not matter if a Web site has great information if you have to spend all afternoon trying to find it. Does the site have an internal search engine? A site map?

- Is the information complete? Does the site seem to have all the information you want on a given subject, or do you have to visit other sites for related information? If you do have to go offsite for information, remember to review the linked site's credibility. One credible site that links to another site does not guarantee the credibility of the second site.

- Is the information substantive? Often Web sites just skim the surface of legal topics. The best sites have in-depth information that tells you more than you already know. They also have free substantive information. Some sites hint at their contents and then make you pay to see the full document. In general, the Web offers so much free information that you should not have to pay. When information is hard to find or its credibility is hard to determine, then you might want to go to Westlaw or Lexis. Much information for sale on the Web is available as part of the vast Westlaw and Lexis databases.

Technology

To evaluate a site's technology, ask a few questions.

- Is the site easy to get around, or navigate? No matter how good the information, if figuring out how to get from one page to another frustrates you, you do not want to select that site as a favorite.

- Is the site well maintained? Well maintained sites have links that go to their intended places and time-sensitive information that is kept up to date. If the site is frequently unavailable or slow, that may indicate inadequate maintenance.

- Is the site design useful? Although you are probably not a Web designer, you can still tell whether a site is well designed. Design reflects the organization of the information on the site and the way you move around. Design also addresses issues like color and the appropriate use of graphics and animation. If the color contrast makes the text difficult to read or a flashing advertisement prevents you from concentrating, the site probably has some design issues.

Exercise
4-2

Begin compiling your own list of favorite sites by answering the questions in Exercise 4-2 at the end of the chapter.

State Law Library

Few people know more about legal research than your state law librarian. If your state law library has a Web page, it may be an excellent source of information about online legal research in your state. You can probably link to it from your state's home page. For a great example, check out the Washington State Law Library at **http://www.wa.gov/courts/lawlib/home.htm**.

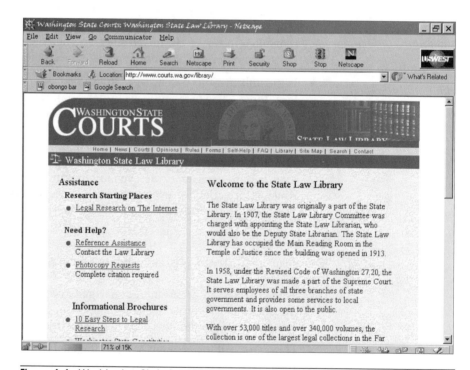

Figure 4-4: Washington State Law Library. *From www.courts.wa.gov/library.*

Free Versus Paid

This chapter discussed the skills needed to do legal research on the Internet. It also looked at the strengths and weaknesses of information the Internet provides. However, the chapter has not yet covered when to use the Internet instead of a paid legal database. You must make this determination on a case-by-case basis. As you become more familiar with the resources available, you will figure out which tools you like using to find different types of information. Many exercises in this text encourage you to try the same exercise using several different sources so that you can get a feel for which works better for each different task. Avoid taking the lazy way and always starting at the same point without thinking about the kind of information you are looking for. Just a few minutes of strategizing may save you several minutes or even hours of research frustration.

SUMMARY

The World Wide Web provides the legal researcher with a vast array of resources for effective legal research. The biggest problem is finding the information. This chapter looked at the various search tools available—search engines, directories, meta search tools, and the like—and compared their functions.

The chapter also described how to search for information. Stressing that the same strategies can be used regardless of the source, the chapter presented some strategies that focus specifically on Internet research.

After finding the information, evaluating its credibility is important. Simply being aware of credibility issues helps, but asking a couple of questions about reliability can insure that your efforts are not based on bad information.

Searching for information on the Web can be challenging. As a skilled researcher, you should create a list of sites that facilitate finding information quickly. This chapter discusses how to create such a list and how to make sure your choices are among the best.

This chapter is just an introduction to doing legal research on the Internet. Throughout the chapters in the second part of the text, you will practice the skills you learned in this chapter so that, in the end, you will be an effective electronic legal researcher, regardless of the information sources.

Notes

1. Top ranking organizations include Media Matrix and NetRatings.
2. For more detail on this and for additional information on how to search the Web, visit Search Engine Watch (**www.searchenginewatch.com**).
3. A person who wants to appeal a decision made by an administrative agency must first exhaust their administrative remedies by going through the procedural hurdles set up by the agency. Only after exhausting administrative remedies can the party access the court.

EXERCISES

Exercise 4-1

Use the Internet to answer the questions in this exercise.

1. Go to the general search engine of your choice and, without looking at its specific search options, type the query: *exhaustion of remedies*.[3] What are the results?

2. Look at the detailed search information for that Web site. (You can usually find it under a Help link.) Does it contain information that you can use to make this search query more effective while using this same search tool?

3. Try the exhaustion of remedies search again. This time, use strategies suggested in this chapter. Are the results you receive different?

4. Try to browse for the same information. Go to a non-legal directory, and see if you can gather similar information about exhaustion of remedies. Identify each step of your search. For example, (1) went to Yahoo!, (2) selected the government category, (3) selected legal—and so on, until you reach a dead end or find the material.

5. Use the same browsing technique with a law-specific directory like FindLaw. Do the number and usefulness of your steps differ?

Exercise 4-2

Use the set of site evaluation worksheets at the end of the chapter to complete this exercise.

1. Use the site evaluation worksheet to determine why these three legal research sites are so popular.

   • Hieros Gamos (**www.hg.org**)
   • Cornell Law School (**www.law.cornell.edu**)
   • Law.com (**www.law.com**)

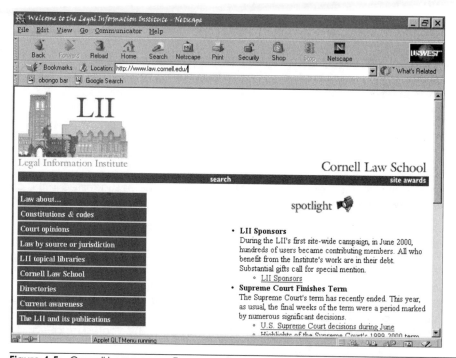

Figure 4-5: Cornell home page. *From www.law.cornell.edu. Used with the permission of the Legal Information Institute, Cornell Law School.*

2. Use skills that you learned in this chapter to find and evaluate three more legal research sites. You may wish to focus on sites with legal information specific to your state. Be sure to pick sites that are not mentioned in this text.

Chapter Review Exercises:

Answer the questions below using Internet resources. If appropriate, use a research strategy like the Five Questions to assist your research.

1. Gabriella recently bought a piece of property with an easement across one corner, permitting public access to a stream. The stream has been dry for years, and it appears to Gabriella that no one has used the easement for a long time. Now, Gabriella wants to put a garden room on a portion of the easement. What steps does she need to take to do this?

2. Your attorney is drafting a lease for a corporate client. She wants to include a clause that would require the parties to go to mediation if a dispute arises under the contract. Can you suggest some language?

3. Lucy and several other volunteers were on a charter flight to a small Latin American nation where they were to work as missionaries. There was great political unrest in the country, and all the volunteers were very nervous. The in-flight movie was about a group of missionaries who were brutally killed during political unrest. The movie upset Lucy very much, causing her to suffer from insomnia for weeks, eventually abandon her mission, and return home only a few weeks after arriving. Lucy wants to sue the airline for intentional infliction of emotional distress. Are the elements for that tort met in this situation?

4. Your attorney is interested in comparing the language of the Uniform Commercial Code on the Statute of Frauds to the Statute of Frauds language adopted by your state. Can you find the two sections?

5. You volunteer with a nonprofit organization that delivers legal services to the poor. The organization decides to collect some Web resources to help their pro se clients. Can you suggest three or four high quality Web sites? Be sure to review the sites carefully for useful content. You may find the Web site evaluation worksheet helpful for answering this question.

Worksheet

Web Site Evaluation Worksheet

Name of Site _____

Site address _____

For the following information, use a scale of 0–2 for a high score of 14.

> 0=bad
> 1=good
> 2=very good

Information

Is the information credible?   Score ____

Comments:

Is the information easy to find?   Score ____

Comments:

Is the information complete?   Score ____

Comments:

Is the information substantive?   Score ____

Comments:

Technology

Is the site easy navigate?   Score _____

Comments:

Is the site well maintained?   Score _____

Comments:

Is the site well designed?   Score _____

Comments:

Worksheet

Search Engine Comparison

Name and Site Address: Alta Vista (**www.altavista.com**) Search engine plus basic directory using LookSmart

Search Options: **Natural language** question search. **Simple search** uses + and – and quotation marks. Permits searching in foreign languages, as well as specific image, audio, and video searching. **Advanced search** incorporates Boolean searching with either words or symbols. Also permits date limitations.

Comments:

Name and Site Address: Ask Jeeves (**www.ask.com**) Meta search tool

Search Options: **Natural language** question search. Supports quotation phrase searching.

Comments:

Name and Site Address: Dogpile (**www.dogpile.com**) Meta search tool plus directory

Search Options: **Simple search** allows for quotation and parentheses phrase searching. It searches three search engines at a time until it finds at least ten hits. Permits specific image, audio, and news searching.

Comments:

Name and Site Address: Excite (**www.excite.com**) Directory

Search Options: **Simple search** uses + and – searching, as well as the "more like this" option for searching results. **Advanced search** is in a form that permits Boolean-like exclusions and inclusions, adult language filter, as well as language, country, and domain limits. Has separate advanced audio/video search and newsgroup search.

Comments:

Name and Site Address: Google (**www.google.com**) Search Engine

Search Options: **Simple search** defaults to all words. Automatically orders relevance of searches. Super simple interface.

Comments:

Name and Site Address: HotBot (**www.hotbot.com**) Search engine plus directory

Search Options: **Simple search** lets you choose any words, all words, exact phrase, page title, person, URL links, and Boolean. Also allows time limits and requests for the inclusion of images, video, MP3, and JavaScript. **Advanced search** is in a form that allows the above with greater functionality, plus foreign language searching, word stemming (multiple word endings), and domain restrictions.

Comments:

Name and Site Address: Mamma (**www.mamma.com**) Meta search tool

Search Options: **Simple search** allows + and – operators, as well as news, MP3, audio, image, and video searching over eight search engines. **Power search** allows for phrase searching as well as a limit to the search engines used.

Comments:

Name and Site Address: Metacrawler (**www.metacrawler.com**) Meta search tool plus directory

Search Options: **Simple search** allows for any, all, and phrase searching, as well as Web and newsgroup limitations. **Power search** allows for limitations on search engines used and limits location of Web site.

Comments:

Name and Site Address: Northern Light (**www.northernlight.com**) Search Engine

Search Options: **Simple search** supports natural language searching. It also allows for full Boolean searching, field limitations (title, URL, etc.), source limitations. **Power search** form eases title, URL, and publication search. Also allows limitations of topic, document type, language, country, and date. Includes the highly useful US Government Search.

Comments:

Name and Site Address: Webcrawler (**www.webcrawler.com**) Directory

Search Options: **Simple search** supports natural language searching. **Advanced search** uses Boolean operators

Comments:

Name and Site Address: Yahoo! (**www.yahoo.com**) Directory

Search Options: **Simple search** allows +, −, and quotation term indicators. **Advanced search** allows all, any, and phrase matching. **Advanced search** syntax allows Boolean search operators.

Comments:

Worksheet

Specialty Search Tools Useful to the Legal Researcher

Name and Site Address: FindLaw (**www.findlaw.com**) Directory

Search Options: Broad directory includes site all over the Web and a large quantity of proprietary information. **Simple search** uses Boolean AND, OR, NEAR (10 words), and NOT.

Comments:

Name and Site Address: LawCrawler (**www.lawcrawler.com**) Search engine

Search Options: Searches Web sites with legal information and is powered by Alta Vista. **Simple search** uses Boolean AND, OR, NEAR (10 words), and NOT.

Comments:

Name and Site Address: The Law Engine (**www.thelawengine.com**) Directory

Search Options: Straightforward one-page format to browse through topics

Comments:

Name and Site Address: The Legal Engine (**www.thelegalengine.com**) Directory

Search Options: Easy-to-use directory links you to major law sources on the Net. Works with FindLaw.

Comments:

Worksheet

Internet Research Toolbox

Use this worksheet to comment on the Web sites featured in this chapter and to include information on your favorites.

Website: Google (**www.google.com**)

Favorite Features:

Comments:

Website: Alta Vista (**www.altavista.com**)

Favorite Features:

Comments:

Website: Northern Light (**www.northernlight.com**)

Favorite Features:

Comments:

Website: Excite (**www.excite.com**)

Favorite Features:

Comments:

Website: Yahoo! (**www.yahoo.com**)

Favorite Features:

Comments:

Website: Webcrawler (**www.webcrawler.com**)

Favorite Features:

Comments:

Website: Infoseek (**www.infoseek.com**)

Favorite Features:

Comments:

Website: Metacrawler (**www.metacrawler.com**)

Favorite Features:

Comments:

Website: FindLaw (**www.findlaw.com**)

Favorite Features:

Comments:

Website: Dogpile (**www.dogpile.com**)

Favorite Features:

Comments:

Website: Ask Jeeves (**www.ask.com**)

Favorite Features:

Comments:

Website: Washington State law Library (**www.wa.gov/courts/lawlib/home.htm**)

Favorite Features:

Comments:

What to Search For

5

Finding and Understanding Statutes

Chapter Objectives

- **Review of statutory law:** What are statutes? How do they differ from regulations and other kinds of law?
- **Statute search strategies:** Depending on the information you have to start with, there are different strategies for finding a statute when you have a citation, a statute name, or a topic.
- **Statutory interpretation:** After finding the statutes, you often need to interpret them to complete your research. In this chapter, you learn the basic rules of statutory interpretation.

On the Web:

- Annotated links leading you to:
  - How a bill becomes a law
  - The federal legal system
  - How to research legislative history
- Exercises for additional help

Review of Statutory Law

Statute
also known as an act or code. A law created by the legislative branch of government.

Act
see statute.

Statutes, or **acts**, are broad pronouncements of law created by legislative bodies at the federal or state level. When searching for statutes, you must be aware of several basic issues of legal research.

First, you must clearly understand the difference between state and federal law. Sometimes state and federal laws have similar names and regulate in similar ways. For example, Pennsylvania has the *Banking Code of 1965*, 7 P.S. §101, *et seq*. To confuse you, the federal government has the *Banking Act of 1933*, 12 USC 227. So, you can see why knowing whether you are looking for state or federal law is important. If you look in the federal code for a state law, you will not succeed any time soon.

Next, you need to make sure that what you want is a statute and not a regulation or case law. Determining the difference is often hard, but keep the following in mind.

- Statutes are generally broad, while regulations are detailed, filling in the specifics of the broad statutory pronouncements. (For more information on regulations, see Chapter 7.)

- Statutes authorize regulations.

- Congress or your state legislature creates statutes. Administrative agencies create regulations.

- Statutes often contain the word *Act*, as in the Clean Air Act.

Once you are certain you are looking for a statute, keep in mind that most statutes have several sections. When you search documents in an electronic format, each section registers as a hit. So, if you look for the Clean Air Act, for example, you get dozens of hits, indicating each separate section of the act. If the Clean Air Act has fifty sections, you get at least fifty hits, all of which are correct. If you do a search based on the act's title, you can narrow your search by using the name of the act, plus keywords specific to what you are looking for in the act. For example:

"Clean Air Act" AND permit NEAR emission

Another important thing to remember when researching statutes is that an administrative agency enforces most statutes. For example, the Environmental Protection Agency enforces the Clean Air Act. You can often guess which agency might enforce a statute from the subject matter. Knowing the enforcing agency is helpful because it might give you more options for doing your research. For example, many agencies post the full text of laws they enforce on their Web sites, along with helpful explanatory materials in plain English. Visit the text Web pages for links to several federal and state agencies.

Statute Search Strategies

Finding statutory law electronically can be challenging—especially if you are used to researching "by the book." Books let you to browse through a statute, flip pages, and generally stumble around until you find what you are looking for. Since statutes tend to be long and contain several parts, stumbling around can be a very useful way to go. Unfortunately, electronic resources are not as stumble friendly. To succeed in searching most electronic resources for a statute, you really need to know what you are looking for.

You can sometimes mimic flipping pages by browsing through an electronic table of contents. Browsing is particularly helpful if you know the name of the law you are looking for or if you would know it when you see it. Browsing also gives you the advantage of a book—you can look through a table of contents to see what might be there. When you find what you need or get better keywords, you can do a more specific search if needed. As you will learn later in the chapter, not all electronic resources allow browsing, so you want to become familiar with those that offer this useful feature.

When looking for a statute, you generally have at least one of these pieces of information:

- citation
- statute name
- topic

The next section explores how to find a statute using those pieces of information with paid legal databases and on the Internet.

Research Strategies

Before you begin your statute search, ask these questions:

♦ Do I really want a statute?
♦ Do I want a state or federal statute?
♦ Which agency might enforce the statute?

Finding Statutes with Citations

Citation
abbreviated method of referring to a source of information. Found in both legal and non-legal documents, citations follow a specific format. In legal writing, the main resource for legal citation format is the Bluebook.

Code
see statute.

Finding a statute with a **citation** is the best of all possible research positions. From the citation, you can easily tell whether you are searching for state or federal law. Almost all federal statutes are in the United States Code (USC). Locations of state citations vary, but their titles often include the word *code*, *statute*, or *laws*. For example, Oklahoma has the Oklahoma Statutes (OS), and West Virginia has the West Virginia Code (WVC).

Westlaw Searching

Westlaw's Find tool makes pulling up a document easy when you know the citation. Simply choose Find a Document, and type the citation. When using Westlaw, keep in mind that you do not have to use periods or other proper citation indicators to access the requested document. For example, you could shorten 33 U.S.C. §151 to *33 usc 151* and still locate the document.

Make sure that you enter your citation in the right place. Frequently students enter a citation in the regular Westlaw search box. While this does find your statute, it also finds cross-references to it—dozens of generally frustrating hits. If cross-references are what you want, this is a great way to get them, but if you are just searching for a single statute section, Find is the way to go.

You can easily use the Find function in Westlaw.com by entering your citation in the *Find This Document By Citation* box on the Welcome page under Rapid Research or from within Westlaw.com's Start menu. Whether you use the dial-up or Internet version of Westlaw, you'll discover finding a document with the citation is a fairly simple activity.

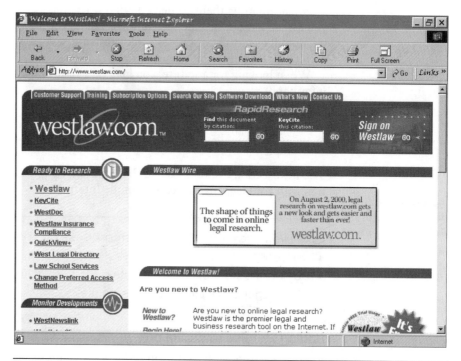

Figure 5-1: You can quickly find a document using the Rapid Research feature on the Westlaw.com home page. *From the Westlaw Web site, www.westlaw.com. Used with the permission of West Group.*

Lexis Searching

Lexis has a tool called Lexstat that lets you quickly and easily pull up a statute with a citation. When using Lexstat, keep in mind that you do not have to use periods or other proper citation indicators. For example, you could shorten *33 U.S.C. §151* to *33 usc 151* and get the same results.

Frequently students do not enter their citations in the proper place. They enter a citation in the regular Lexis search box. They find their statutes and dozens of cross-references. This is a great method for finding cross-references, but an ineffi-cient way to search for a single statute section. Lexstat is the way to go.

You can easily access the Lexstat function under the Legal Services tab in Lexis or the Get a Document tab in Lexis.com. From there, you enter your citation, making sure to indicate that your choice is a statute, not case law or a law review article.

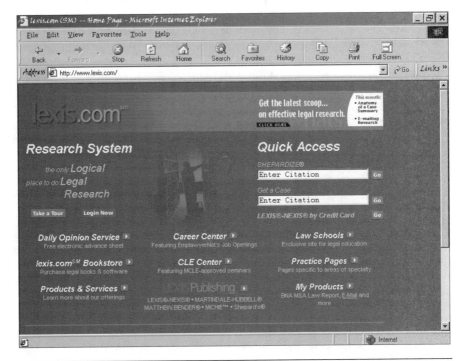

Figure 5-2: Lexis makes it easy to get documents by citation directly from its home page. *Reprinted with the permission of LEXIS-NEXIS, a division of Reed Elsevier Inc. Lexis-Nexis, Lexis, Nexis, the Information Array logo and lexis.com are registered trademarks of Reed Elsevier Properties Inc., used with the permission of LEXIS-NEXIS.*

Loislaw Searching

In Loislaw, you can get a statute with the citation by selecting the proper data-base and choosing the Advanced Search option. From there, enter your citation in the Official Citation space. Be careful to use the correct citation format: Loislaw is not as forgiving as Westlaw and Lexis.

CD Law Searching

CD Law has no special tool for finding a document by citation. This is common in smaller databases because there is less to search. Fortunately, smaller databases do often have a Table of Contents feature. You can browse through CD Law's Table of Contents feature or enter the citation using Boolean search operators.

Internet Searching

Several law-related search tools let you search a limited USC database with a citation. One such site is FindLaw (**www.findlaw.com**).[1] This tool is not as exact as those of paid legal databases, but it works well. Your search will yield lots of results, since it may bring up cross-references. Try searching your citation as a phrase to get better results.

Browsing is also available on many Internet sites. Remember, statutes often have several sections. You may have a statute reference that notes only the beginning section. For example, 23 USC 453, *et sec. **Et seq** means and all the following sections.* When this is the case, your citation takes you to the beginning of the statute. Unfortunately, what you need may be somewhere within the statute. If so, try browsing through the table of contents to find relevant information.

Browsing in a paid legal database can be complicated, but some Web sites make it pretty easy. Try the Legal Information Institute Web page at Cornell Law School (**www.law.cornell.edu**).[2] From there, you can select the appropriate title and browse around the sections until you find what you need. Related CFR sections, updates, and topical references make this site a must for your toolbox of favorite sites.

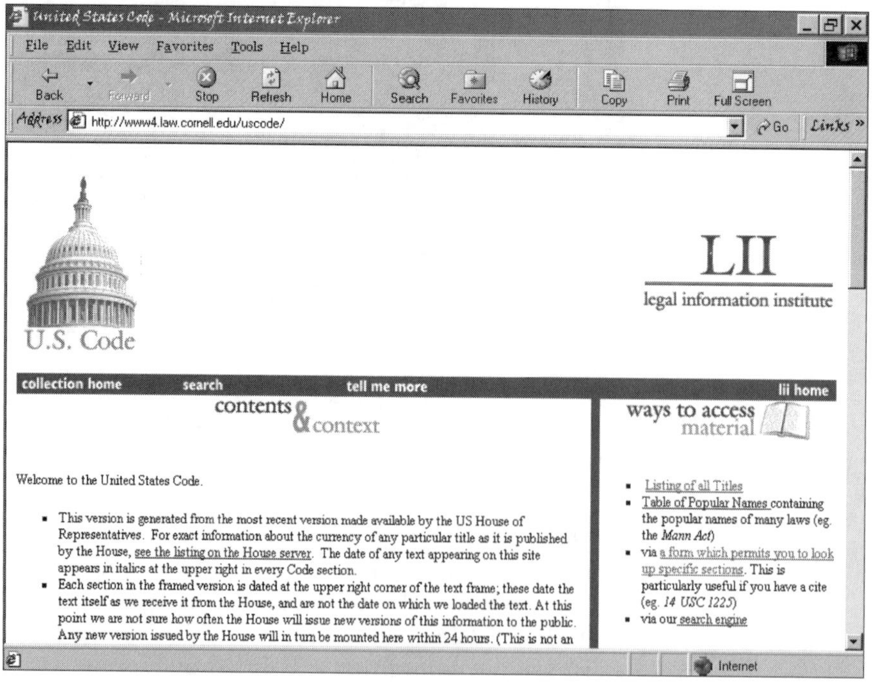

Et seq

Latin phrase meaning *all the following sections.* Statutory citations often use this phrase where the first section of the statute is cited and the rest are included.

Figure 5-3: You can search the United States Code on the Cornell Law School site. *From www.law.cornell.edu. Used with the permission of the Legal Information Institute, Cornell Law School.*

Exercise 5-1

Practice finding statutes with a citation by completing Exercise 5-1 at the end of this chapter.

Finding Statutes with a Name

When you only have a statute name, you generally use more traditional, Boolean-style searching. Try using phrase searching or segment searching for better results.

Westlaw Searching

Field-restricted search
in Westlaw, a search of specific portions of a document like the title, author, parties, etc.

If you know the title of the statute, you can do what is known as a **field-restricted search** in the Query dialog box. To do this, open the Query dialog box and pick the Find By Title tab.

If you are using a regular Query dialog box to do the search, remember to select the proper database. Remember, you cannot find what you are looking for if you look in the wrong database. To narrow your search, you can use other relevant keywords as part of your title search. Depending on the database you choose, you get not only the statute but also supporting and referring documents. For example, if you are looking for the Endangered Species Act and your focus is the meaning of the word *habitat*, you might try the query:

"Endangered Species Act" AND habitat

Lexis Searching

Segment searching
in Lexis, a search of specific portions of a document, such as the title, author, parties, etc.

Lexis offers two ways to do a name search. Using the first method, **segment searching**, you search individual segments of a document. For example, you can search the title, the citation, the date, and so on. In this situation, you search the title segment, since you know the name, or title, of the statute. Even when you use segment searching, you can use additional keywords, connecting them with the usual Boolean operators.

You can also do a general search and use quotation marks around the statute name (*"Endangered Species Act"*). This searches for the title of the act anywhere within the text of the documents.

Do not forget to select the proper database. Remember, you cannot find what you are looking for if you look in the wrong database. To narrow your search, you can use other relevant keywords. Depending on the database you choose, you get not only the statute but also supporting and referring documents. For example, if you are looking for the Endangered Species Act and your focus is the meaning of the word *habitat*, you might try the query:

"Endangered Species Act" AND habitat

Loislaw Searching

In Loislaw, you can search for a statute by name by selecting the proper database and choosing the Advanced Search option. Then, enter the statute name in the Title space.

CD Law Searching

In CD Law, the Table of Contents feature again comes in handy as a quick way to browse for a statute by name. Alternatively, enter the title in the normal search box using Boolean search operators.

Internet Searching

If you have the name of the act and you are doing an Internet search, you may want to try some strategizing before you search. Many agencies at the federal level post their statutes on their Web pages. Since an agency administers most federal acts, going to the agency's Web page can be the easiest way to find the act you want. You might also discover explanatory documents in plain English. Use the Web site's internal search tool (if it has one), and try placing quotation marks around the act's title to facilitate your search. Even if the agency's Web site does not have the actual text of the statute you want, it might have discussions about the act that contain useful citations that can help you do a more direct search.

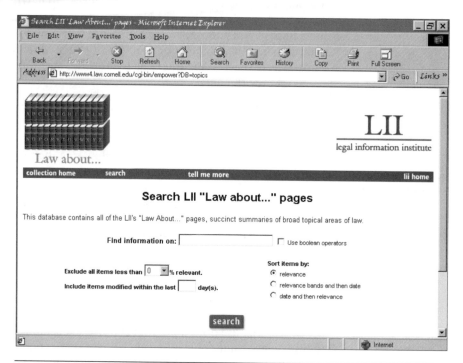

Figure 5-4: Cornell internal search. Use internal Web site search tools when available. *From www.law.cornell.edu. Used with the permission of the Legal Information Institute, Cornell Law School.*

Exercises 5-2 and 5-3

Practice finding a statute with a name by answering the questions in Exercises 5-2 and 5-3 at the end of the text.

Finding Statutes with a Topic

Finding a statute when you only have a topic generally requires traditional Boolean-style searching. So choosing good keywords and searching the appropriate databases are important. Before you start your search, clearly identify whether your statute is a state or federal law. Remember that your search can only succeed when you do it in the right place.

Guided Exercise: Westlaw or Lexis Searching

Once you select the appropriate database, you use your basic Westlaw or Lexis skills to find the statute itself.[3] Let's look at an example.

> *Our client, Maryanne Gato has been a connoisseur of fine wines for many years. Recently, she decided to open her own winery. She believes that wine labels are subject to federal regulation, and she wants your firm to find the specifics of those regulations. Your job is to find the relevant statute.*

1. **Determine whether the law is a state or federal law.** You have been told that the law is federal.

2. **Identify appropriate databases.** Here, simply choosing the United States Code Annotated (USCA) is your best bet. Remember to start with the narrowest database.

3. **Brainstorm to identify keywords.** For this exercise, you might choose the keywords *wine* and *label*. In forming your query, remember that the word *label* may appear in several forms—*labels, labeling,* and so on. So, here is your query:

   wine and label!

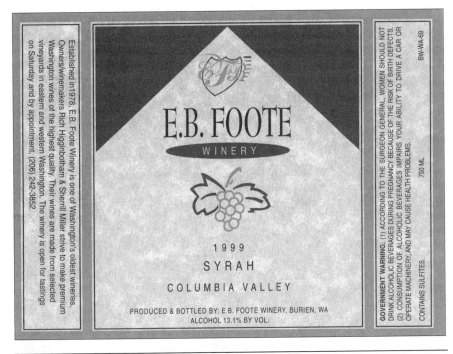

Figure 5-5: E.B. Foote wine label. *Courtesy of E.B. Foote Winery.*

This query yields over 100 documents. Narrow the search using the Westlaw's Locate or Lexis' Focus feature.

wine w/5 label!

This query yields less than 10 documents, one of which is 27 USC§205, the Federal Alcohol Administration Act regarding unfair competition and unlawful practices. Subsection (e) sets labeling requirements.

Guided Exercise—Internet Searching

With Internet searching, strategy again leads the way. Avoid the research trap of searching the entire Web for something that is likely to be in one place. As we know, agencies generally administer statutes.

1. **Use the wine example in the proceeding Guided Exercise.** Answer this question: Which agency would you predict administers laws about wine labels? (Feel free to browse the chart of federal agencies now on the text website.) If you guess the Food and Drug Administration, you are right.

2. **Confirm your answer.** Access the Food and Drug Administration Web site. Try to make an educated guess to determine the site address—**www.fda.gov**.

3. **Get ideas about how to search.** At the FDA Web site, take a moment to look at its search help for ideas about how to search. You see that Boolean searching is the base and that it allows wildcard searching with a question mark (?).

4. Use what you have learned about the FDA site to search with this query:

wine and label?

The search should yield several documents that discuss labeling requirements for wine, including relevant citations. This takes advantage of the backwards search strategy discussed earlier. By looking at secondary source material on the FDA Web site, we find both the relevant statute, as well as information about its enforcement. This is much better information than we would find looking at the statute alone. With the citation, we can visit a site like Findlaw to look up the actual statute.

Statutory Interpretation

When you find your statute, you may then need to determine its meaning. To do this, you use the rules of statutory interpretation. The first rule of statutory interpretation is to look to the plain meaning of the statute, that is, ask yourself what the statute seems to mean on its face. As you can imagine, the plain meaning is not always so plain. The Federal Endangered Species Act is a good example. This law prevents the taking of an endangered species. Read the following statutory language:

> **16 USC 1538 Prohibited Acts....** *(W)ith respect to any endangered species of fish or wildlife listed pursuant to section 1533 of this title it is unlawful for any person subject to the jurisdiction of the United States to–*
>
> *(B)* **take** *any such species within the United States or the Territorial sea of the United States; ...*

You may ask what it means to take an endangered species. The plain meaning might lead you to believe that take means to pick up the species and remove it from its habitat. If so, you would only be partially correct. Thus, it is important that legal researchers not assume they know what important terms mean. So, how can you determine what a word really means? Well, one step is to look at the legislation itself. Statutes frequently include definitions sections that explain the meanings of potentially confusing words.

> **16 USC 1532(19) Definitions.** *The term "take" means to harass, harm, pursue, hunt, shoot, wound, kill, trap, capture, or collect, or to attempt to engage in any such conduct.*

Another option is to look to the regulations related to the statute; they often contain definitions and explanations that clarify the statute. In this example, the Department of the Interior created regulatory definitions for the Endangered Species Act.[4]

> **50 CFR §17.3 Definitions.** *Harass in the definition of "take" in the Act means an intentional or negligent act or omission which creates the likelihood of injury to wildlife by annoying it to such an extent as to significantly disrupt normal behavioral patterns which include, but are not limited to, breeding, feeding, or sheltering. This definition, when applied to captive wildlife, does not include generally accepted:*
>
> *(1) Animal husbandry practices that meet or exceed the minimum standards for facilities and care under the Animal Welfare Act,*
>
> *(2) Breeding procedures, or*
>
> *(3) Provisions of veterinary care for confining, tranquilizing, or anesthetizing, when such practices, procedures, or provisions are not likely to result in injury to the wildlife.*

> *Harm in the definition of "take" in the Act means an act which actually kills or injures wildlife. Such act may include significant habitat modification or degradation where it actually kills or injures wildlife by significantly impairing essential behavioral patterns, including breeding, feeding or sheltering.*

A third option is to look to case law, which may interpret the meaning of the confusing section as well. A little research on this issue reveals that the main case on this matter is *Babbit v Sweet Home*, 515 U.S. 687 (1995). In the *Babbit* case, the Sweet Home Chapter of Communities for a Great Oregon challenged the authority of the Secretary of the Department of the Interior to include the word *harm* in the definition of the word *take*. The United States Supreme Court confirmed that it was reasonable for the Secretary to create such a definition. In this excerpt from the case, the court looks at the legislative history for you.

> *Our conclusion that the Secretary's definition of "harm" rests on a permissible construction of the ESA gains further support from the legislative history of the statute. The Committee Reports accompanying the bills that became the ESA do not specifically discuss the meaning of "harm," but they make clear that Congress intended "take" to apply broadly to cover indirect as well as purposeful actions. The Senate Report stressed that "'take' is defined ... in the broadest possible manner to include every conceivable way in which a person can 'take' or attempt to 'take' any fish or wildlife." S. Rep. No. 93-307, p. 7 (1973). The House Report stated that "the broadest possible terms" were used to define restrictions on takings. H. R. Rep. No. 93-412, p. 15 (1973). The House Report underscored the breadth of the "take" definition by noting that it included "harassment, whether intentional or not." Id., at 11 (emphasis added).[5]*

Legislative history
documentation of the process that a bill went through to become a law. Often used to interpret the law after its passage.

If you look at those three sources and still do not know what your confusing section means, it is time to turn to legislative history. **Legislative history** is a collection of documents that record the entire process of a bill's becoming law, from its first presentation to the legislature, through committee, to its final vote, to signing by the President or to the legislature's override of a veto. Given all this useful information, you may wonder why legislative history appears to be a last resort. The main reason is that legislative history can be complicated, confusing, and frustrating. Fortunately, the average researcher does not need to research legislative history very often. Because of that, this chapter does not discuss how to research legislative history. However, Appendix A contains more information on how to do it, including four simple steps to get started.

SUMMARY

Searching for statutes gives you the opportunity to use all your research skills. No matter what piece of information you have to begin with, you can find the relevant statute. After determining that a statute is really what you want and after confirming the appropriate jurisdiction, you can find statutes with a citation, the statute title, or a topic or keywords.

After finding your statute, you may need to determine its meaning. Courts usually look first to the plain meaning of a statute, but actually understanding the meaning of a statute generally takes more than a simple reading of the law. Understanding simple rules of statutory interpretation can help you make initial determinations to aid your analysis.

Notes

1. Statutes on Findlaw at *http://www.findlaw.com/casecode/code.html*.
2. Cornell Law School Statutes section at *http://www.law.cornell.edu/uscode/*.
3. You may also do this exercise using Loislaw with slight modifications. CD law does not have federal statutes.
4. It is frequently believed that the Environmental Protection Agency is the lead agency on the Endangered Species Act. This is not the case. The United States Fish and Wildlife Service, a section of the Department of the Interior, maintains the list of over 600 endangered species. For general information on the Endangered Species Program, visit *http://endangered.fws.gov/*.
5. *Babbit v Sweet Home*, 525 U.S. 687, p. 704 (1995).

EXERCISES

Exercise 5-1

You often have more than one resource for finding the information you need. The skilled researcher knows the faster way to find the best information. Determine the faster way to find a statute with a citation using this exercise.

1. Look up the following citations using the Internet and a paid legal database.

2. Using your personal research standards, indicate the pros and cons of each search method in the space provided.

Citation	Paid Legal Database		Internet	
	Pros	Cons	Pros	Cons
42 USC 1201				
16 USC 1151				
21 USC 1054				
42 USC 14301				

Exercise 5-2

Find the following statutes at both the state and the federal levels. Your state act's name might differ slightly—ask your instructor for clarification.

1. Use both the paid legal database and the Internet for your search.

2. Note the proper starting citation when you find the act.

3. Note the pros and cons of each method of searching.

Citation	Paid Legal Database		Internet	
	Pros	*Cons*	*Pros*	*Cons*
Clean Water Act Cite:				
Public Records Act Cite:				
Community Reinvestment Act Cite:				
Battered Women's Testimony Act Cite:				

Exercise 5-3

To complete this exercise, answer the following questions.

1. Are your state's statutes available online? Where?

2. Are the statutes searchable? Browsable? Or both?

3. Ask your instructor to give you some citations to look up, and try to make the same comparison that you did in the Exercise 5-2.

Where are your state's materials located on the paid legal database?

Which statutory materials are located there?

	Paid Legal Database		**Internet—State Site**	
Citation	*Pros*	*Cons*	*Pros*	*Cons*
Cite:				
Cite:				
Cite:				
Cite:				

Chapter Review Exercises:

Answer each of the following questions, and include a statutory citation to support your answer. You can find the appropriate statutes using the statute finding worksheets at the end of this chapter.

1. Our client, Pestly Pesticides, Inc., manufactures pesticides that are exported to Latin American countries. Can the labels warning workers of the dangers of the product be in English?

2. Allison Green is curious about what types of disabilities the Americans with Disabilities Act covers. What is the citation for that act?

3. Reading the local paper, Cheedy Jaja notices that the federal Department of Transportation recently held a meeting in his neighborhood regarding rail traffic. He wants to see the minutes and to read participants' testimony. He believes this is public information. Is it?

4. Dissident Gavin Smith just finished his first novel, and he is convinced it will take the world by storm. He wants to copyright it, but he does not want the hassle of working with the government. Does he need to go through the Copyright Office to copyright the book?

Worksheet

Statute Finding Worksheet

Complete the worksheet before you begin researching.

Starting information: Fill in unknown information as you find it.

Statute citation

Statute name

Statute topic/area of law

Initial questions

Is it state or federal?

What agency might administer this statute?

Am I sure that it is a statute that I am looking for? Why?

Tracking Information: From the keywords and other information you have, plot your strategy for finding the statute. What will be your first step and why? Complete this section of the worksheet before you actually begin the research, then record how it worked. (Do not worry if you do not take the exact number of steps listed in the worksheet—feel free to use the back of the worksheet to list more steps. If you can complete the task in fewer steps, celebrate your improved research skills!)

Step One:

Plan:

How Did It Work?

Step Two:

Plan:

How Did It Work?

Step Three:

Plan:

How Did It Work?

Step Four:

Plan:

How Did It Work?

Step Five:

Plan:

How Did It Work?

Worksheet

Statute Research Toolbox

Use this worksheet to comment on the websites listed and to include information on your favorites.

Website: Westlaw (**www.westlaw.com**)

Favorite Features:

Comments:

Website: Lexis (**www.lexis.com**)

Favorite Features:

Comments:

Website: Loislaw (**www.loislaw.com**)

Favorite Features:

Comments:

Website: CD Law (**www.cdlaw.com**)

Favorite Features:

Comments:

Website: Food and Drug Administration (**www.fda.gov**)

Favorite Features:

Comments:

Website: Legal Information Institute (**www.law.cornell.edu**)

Favorite Features:

Comments:

Website: FindLaw (**www.findlaw.com**)

Favorite Features:

Comments:

6

Finding and Understanding Regulations

Chapter Objectives

- **Review of administrative agencies:** What are regulations? Why you would look to them in legal research?
- **Review of the rule-making process:** Agencies go through a multi-step process to create regulations.
- **Regulation search strategy:** When searching for regulations, you start with certain pieces of information. In this chapter, you will explore how to find regulations when you have a citation, an agency name, a regulation name, or a topic.
- **Regulatory guidance search strategy:** Finding regulatory guidance for federal rules is quite manageable using a simple three-step process.

On the Web

- Annotated links leading you to:
  - Federal and state regulations
  - More information on the regulatory process
  - Examples of agency guidance
- Exercises for additional help

Review of Administrative Agencies

Administrative agencies
a part of the executive branch, administrative agencies have the role of being experts in and advising on a particular area.

Administrative agencies, part of the executive branch of government, are responsible for crafting **regulations**. Generally, only the legislative branch can create law. However, legislatures are able to delegate some lawmaking authority to agencies.

Agencies create rules using a basic **rule-making** process. First a **rule** is proposed. Then the rule is published where people are likely to read it. At the federal level, that is the *Federal Register*. Many states also have publications for announcing proposed rules and other important state information. Publication of the proposed rule starts the public comment period. Interested parties can submit comments via letter or e-mail or in person at public meetings. Comment periods generally last from 30 to 60 days.

Regulation
also known as a rule. Laws created by administrative agencies to implement statutes. A regulation must have statutory authority granted by the legislature.

After interested parties submit comments, the agency reviews those comments and determines whether changes to the proposed rule are needed. If the agency makes major changes to the rule based on the comments, then the agency publishes the revised proposed rule and seeks additional comments. If changes are minor, then the agency simply publishes the final rule. Often a lengthy explanation of the rule's background and how the agency anticipates enforcing it accompanies publication of the final rule. This explanation is known as **guidance**, and this chapter discusses it later.

Rule-making
process of creating a rule or regulation. The Administrative Procedures Act (APA) sets out the multi-step process at the federal level.

After a final rule is published, it is eventually **codified**. At the federal level, the rule becomes part of the Code of Federal Regulations (CFR). At the state level, names vary, with some states having different codes for different agencies. This chapter focuses on finding codified regulations at the state and federal level.

Rule
See regulation.

Regulation Search Strategy

Generally, when you need to look for a regulation, you begin with one or more of the following pieces of information:

Federal Register
daily publication issued by the Government Printing Office that includes, among other things, notices on rule making.

- citation
- agency name
- regulation name
- topic

Let's explore the strategies used to find regulations using each one.

Guidance
information an administrative agency gives to help the regulated community comply with regulations.

Finding a Regulation with a Citation

Ideally, you will have a full citation to work with; this is the easiest way to search for information. A citation from the Code of Federal Regulations provides an example. 40 CFR 1501.4 explains the criteria that the Environmental Protection Agency should use to determine whether or not to conduct an environmental impact statement.

Codification
process of organizing laws according to subject.

Regulation with Citation on Westlaw

Finding a federal regulation with a citation on Westlaw could not be simpler. Simply select the Find this Document by Citation button, and enter your citation. Speed your work by omitting the periods in C.F.R.—Westlaw does not need them to find your citation.

On Westlaw.com, you can enter the citation from the home page using Rapid Research. Just type your citation, and click the Go button. Again, exact spacing and punctuation are not a concern.

For state materials on Westlaw or Westlaw.com, select the State Materials database, choose the state, and go to the Administrative and Executive Materials section. From there, you can find the administrative code, if it is available. Note that state sections do not have the simple citation search that federal regulations do.

Regulation with Citation on Lexis

You can find federal regulations easily using Lexstat in Lexis (Legal Services tab) or Lexis.com (get a document). After you enter your citation, be sure to select the Lexstat function by noting that you are selecting a statute or CFR section. Remember that you do not need to enter periods, section signs, or other symbols in the citation box. Lexstat only works for federal regulations. If you are searching for state regulations, use Lexis segment searching while in your state administrative law database to search for the citation of your state regulation.

Regulation with Citation on Loislaw

For a federal regulation, select the National Law Library in Loislaw. Select Advanced Search to use your citation. Note that the title and part of the citation go on different lines.

Regulation with Citation on CD Law

CD law and products like it frequently omit federal regulations from their collection. However, they generally do a great job with state regulations. In CD Law, you can easily search the Washington Administrative Code. Suppose you want to find WAC 16-540-020, the regulation discussing the powers of the Washington Mint Commodity Board. First, you need to select your database. Here, the selection is the Washington Administrative Code. Be aware of the citation entry requirements of your local product. In CD Law, you type the citation, numbers only, in the search box and your citation pops right up. So might other citations that refer to the regulation, but in smaller databases like an administrative code database, that is often not as worrisome as it is in larger databases.

Regulation with Citation on the Internet

You can use a variety of strategies to find regulations on the Internet. One way is to visit a Web site that offers a selection of regulations. Findlaw (**www.findlaw.com**) and the Cornell Law School Web site (**www.law.cornell.edu**) are two good choices, since they include both state and federal citations.

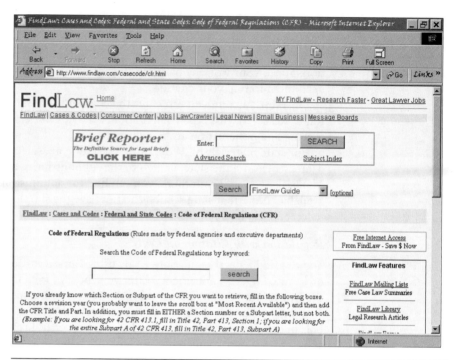

Figure 6-1: The Code of Federal Regulations is available on FindLaw. *From www.findlaw.com.*

Both Cornell and FindLaw lead you to state Web pages with state regulations if the regulations are available on the Internet. In most cases, searching by citation is the easiest way to find the regulation.

Whether searching state or federal regulatory citations, you can also browse for the regulation, especially if you only have a portion of the citation. This feature is generally available under a Table of Contents heading. If you find your title and section that way, they may lead you to what you want.

Another strategy for searching for regulations by citation on the Internet is to visit the Web page of the particular agency, if you know where it is. Many agencies at both the state and federal level post their regulations on their Web sites in both searchable and browsable formats. The advantage of finding your regulation on the agency Web site is that agencies often have general explanations of the regulations in plain English, designed for the **regulated community**. This can be really useful to the researcher, especially if you are unfamiliar with the particular regulation at hand.

For our example, 40 CFR 1501.4, the Environmental Protection Agency is the issuing agency. Go to the EPA Web site (**www.epa.gov**), and select Laws and Regulations. Then select the Code of Federal Regulations link. You can choose the entire CFR or just Title 40. Following our general rule of selecting the narrowest database, select the Title 40 link. Since the citation gives no information on the chapter, use the Table of Contents feature to browse to section 1501.

Regulated community
businesses and individuals subject to an agency's regulations.

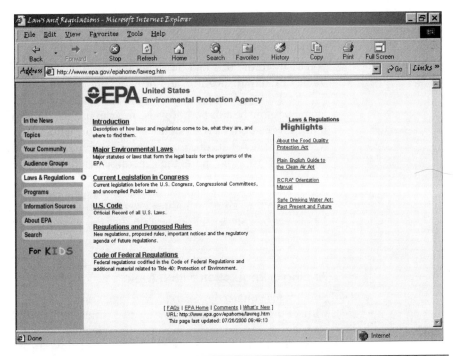

Figure 6-2: EPA regulations. Many agencies post their regulations online. *From www.epa.gov.*

Exercise 6-1

Practice finding regulations by citation by completing Exercise 6-1 at the end of the chapter.

Finding a Regulation with an Agency Name

If you have no citation, but you have a subject and an agency name, you can try two different approaches. The first approach is to access a table of contents and browse to the section that seems most suitable. Sometimes your database has no Table of Contents feature. In that case, you perform a keyword search using the information you have and the skills you learned in the early chapters of this text.

The second approach is to visit the agency's Web site. Many agencies, both at the state and the federal level, post their regulations on their Web pages. As long as you have a topic, you can browse your way to what you need.

Finding a Regulation with Its Name

Doing an ordinary search for a set of regulations by name can be pretty frustrating. The problem is that every single section of a regulation has a heading that contains the regulation's name. If you are fortunate and your regulation only has a few sections, you should have no trouble. More often than not, a regulation has dozens of sections. Using the handy Table of Contents feature is simpler, if one is available. If you have only the regulation's name, do a general search for that name. A quick glance at the first page of your results should lead you easily to the title and the general section. Use that information to go to the Table of Contents feature, and browse your way to the relevant section.

The Table of Contents feature makes online searching more like using a book, giving you the best of both worlds. You can use the Table of Contents feature to find your citation, or you can use it as an information-gathering tool, a guide to narrowing the results of a more general search. If you have the regulation's name and a keyword, you can use the general search function more effectively.

Exercise 6-2

Practice the skills for finding a regulation with the agency name and a subject by completing Exercise 6-2 at the end of the chapter.

Finding a Regulation with a Topic

Sometimes you need to search for a regulation and have only a topic to start with. If that is the case, you can try two different approaches. Start the easy way, with a general search in a specific regulatory directory, using your keyword. If this yields too many results, do a little investigating to find the agency. Often you can guess the correct agency from the topic. You can also use the first page or two of results from your general search to get ideas about the key agency. Once you know the agency, visit its Web site for more specific information to assist you in your search. The Web page could even lead you to the exact citation, or better yet, the regulation itself.

Jurisdiction as referred to in this chapter, indicates whether a regulation falls under state or federal law.

If you have only a topic, and you are not certain of the **jurisdiction**, your search is even more challenging. The best thing to do is to ask the person who assigned you the question (i.e., your teacher or supervising attorney) for more jurisdictional information. If that doesn't work, you can use a few different approaches.

First, use common sense to narrow the jurisdiction as much as possible. Remember that states tend to address some topics and other topics tend to fall under federal jurisdiction. If yours does not neatly fall into one category or another, you need to try a broader approach.

The most effective broad approach might be to search for relevant cases and see if they refer to the regulations you need. Use the general directory of all federal and state cases, and craft the narrowest possible search. Include the terms *regulation or rule* or possibly *agency* to narrow the results to more relevant cases. Case law can be a great backdoor to information. Regulations, like statutes, use specific terms in particular ways; if you don't select just the right term, your search falls flat. Searching cases for regulations can help prevent that problem.

Effective regulatory searches are based on the information you have available. By figuring out what you have and combining the methods described here, you can find regulations quickly, no matter what information you start with.

Figure 6-3: A good strategy is important for effective searching. *Illustration by Joe Mills. Reprinted with permission. All rights reserved.*

Regulatory Guidance Search Strategy

After you find your regulations, you might need to figure out what they mean. If that is the case, turn to regulatory guidance for help. Regulatory guidance consists mainly of comments that accompany the rules at various stages of publication. In that way, it is similar to legislative history but fortunately much easier to access and understand. Some agencies also publish separate guidance or policy documents specifically for the purpose of clarifying confusing rules or explaining the rules' enforcement. Another source of regulatory guidance is agency correspondence written in response to formal requests for regulatory interpretation from members of the regulated community. These combined sources can go a long way towards explaining the meaning of an unclear regulation. As mentioned earlier, finding regulatory guidance is relatively simple compared to finding legislative history. The next section lists the steps that should start you on your way.

Finding Regulatory Guidance

To find most federal regulatory guidance, follow this simple three-step formula:

1. Find the regulation.
2. Look up the relevant *Federal Register* notices.
3. Look for other sources of guidance.

The next section discusses these steps in detail. Remember, this three-step process is designed for research at the federal level. Steps for finding your state's guidance vary, depending on the process your state uses. Many states publish state registers that contain information similar to the *Federal Register*. Thus, the steps described here should be useful in leading you to state guidance as well.

Guided Exercise

Follow the steps below to learn the simple procedure you can use to find regulatory guidance.

1. **Find the regulation.** The first step to understanding what any legal document means is to have that document in front of you. Like statutes, regulations end with valuable information that leads you to the information you need. The National Poultry Improvement Plan, located at 9 CFR 145, *et al.* offers a good example. The next steps look specifically at the general provisions at 9 CFR 145.4.

Figure 6-4: Logo for National Poultry Improvement Plan. *From the Code of Federal Regulations, 9 CFR 145.4.*

2. **Look up the *Federal Register* notices.** At least two *Federal Register* notices are associated with each rule—the proposed rule and the final rule. Quite likely, several more notices are available as well. Look up and read them all. Finding *Federal Register* notices with the citation is easy; you can get them at the end of the regulation.

In our example, 9 CFR 145.4 lists seven *Federal Register* citations (abbreviated as FR). Can you guess which notice relates to the proposed rule? To the final rule? Look up your answers to see if they are right. Hint: Generally, the first notice listed is the proposed rule, and the second notice is the final rule. There are, of course, many exceptions. You can also use a process of elimination to determine which notices are the proposed and final. If the notation says "as amended" or "redesignated at," you know those are changes to the rule, not the original rule.

3. **Look for other sources of guidance.** While the *Federal Register* is the most easily accessible source of federal regulatory guidance, agencies provide guidance in other ways as well. This generally takes the form of specially written guidance documents, policy statements, opinions, and answers to written questions from the regulated community.

Each agency does things slightly differently, of course. As you become familiar with individual agencies, you will become familiar with how each agency shares its vision of how to do things. If you are unfamiliar with the agency from which you are seeking guidance, the best place to start is the agency's Web page. Online, agencies tend to keep their guidance in the same place they keep their regulations, so look for that on the agency home page. Alternatively, search for the words *policy* or *guidance* using the agency's internal search engine.

For our example of the National Poultry Improvement Plan, the appropriate agency is the United States Department of Agriculture (**www.usda.gov**). Visit the agency's Web site, and see if you can find additional information about the National Poultry Improvement Plan. Hint: Search the Web site using a phrase search for the regulation title. Remember to check the search help to use the proper phrase search technique.

Keep an open mind when looking for agency guidance. It can come in many forms: an official document with the title "Agency Guidance," a penalty policy, a formal letter to a member of the regulated community, or an informative brochure on how to comply with the regulation. Any information from the agency that helps you understand the rule and how to comply with it can be categorized as agency guidance.

SUMMARY

Researching regulations is a fairly straightforward process when you are searching electronically. Your search strategy depends on what information you start with. Whether you have the citation, the agency name, the regulation name, or just a topic to work with, you can use that information to find a regulation.

Once you find the regulation, you may be interested in interpreting it. If so, you can investigate agency guidance. Finding guidance is also a relatively straightforward task. Look up the relevant regulation and its register notices, and you will be well on your way to finding useful information about implementing the law.

EXERCISES

Exercise 6-1

1. Look up the following regulations by their citations, using at least two different databases for comparison purposes.

   a. 45 CFR 702.5
   b. 36 CFR 1150.13
   c. 16 CFR 1502.16
   d. GA COMP. R. & REGS. 300-2-5-.02 (Georgia)
   e. Minn. R. 9500.1463 (Minnesota)
   f. 10 NMAC 5.100.8 (New Mexico)

Exercise 6-2

1. Find a citation for the regulations listed below. Remember to use all your research skills in doing this exercise. Do not forget the skills and tools that you learned in the earlier chapters.

   a. Food and Drug Administration enforcement policies (federal)

   b. Legal Services Corporation appeals on behalf of clients (federal)

   c. Fish and Wildlife Service Proceedings for seizure and forfeiture of wildlife (federal)

   d. Arizona Department of Agriculture rules on parlors and milk rooms

e. Maryland Childcare Administration requirements for the home

f. Wyoming Crime Victims Compensation Commission Profits from Crime

Exercise 6-3

1. Find a regulation to answer the following questions regarding federal regulations.

   a. Is it fair practice to use secret coding in market research dealing with silk?

   b. What is the purpose of the Amateur Radio Service?

   c. What is involved in a space-shuttle rendezvous?

2. Find your state's regulations on the following topics. Answer the questions, supporting your answers with the appropriate citations.

   a. Find your state's regulations on getting a license to practice law. Who is eligible?

b. Find your state's regulations on food safety. What is required to get a food handler's card?

c. Find your state's regulations on transportation. Does it include provisions for travel by bicycle?

Exercise 6-4

1. Look on the agency Web sites listed below, and find examples of agency guidance.

2. Note the title of at least one guidance document you find.

   a. Department of Transportation (**www.dot.gov**)

   b. Federal Trade Commission (**www.ftc.gov**)

   c. Food and Drug Administration (**www.fda.gov**) (Look under information for industry.)

Chapter Review Exercises

1. The queries below have different types of information for federal regulations. Figure out what you have, determine a strategy, and find the answers to the questions.

   a. How does the Food and Drug Administration define French dressing?

   b. What is the Literacy Leader Fellowship Program?

   c. What does 22 CFR 1508.100 discuss?

   d. What is the regulatory citation for the hearing procedures for the Merchant Marine Act?

   e. What does 45 CFR 1605.1 discuss?

   f. Where are the regulations for the National Poultry Improvement Plan?

2. Using a favorite news source or an agency's Web site, find a recently finialized regulation, and answer the following questions about it. Support your answers with citations to your sources.

   a. What is the citation of the regulation, and what statute authorizes it?

   b. Why did the agency write the regulation?

   c. Was there much comment during the public comment period? Did the agency modify the proposed rule as a result?

   d. Who does the new regulation impact?

Worksheet

Regulations Location Worksheet

Source: Westlaw

Location: Under the Federal Materials heading, select Administrative Rules and Regulations to find several options for the *Federal Register* (FR), including the Table of Contents feature and an organization by practice area.

Comments:

Source: Lexis

Location: Under Federal Legal, select *Federal Register* (FEDREG).

Comments:

Source: Loislaw

Location: Select the National Lois Library, and, under administrative codes and regulations, select US *Federal Register*.

Comments:

Source: CD Law

Location: Does not have the *Federal Register*, although it does have the *Washington Register* for the State of Washington.

Comments:

Source: Internet

Location: The Government Printing Office maintains the *Federal Register* online. (**http://www.access.gpo.gov/su_docs/aces/aces140.html**) The database dates back to 1995.

Comments:

Worksheet

Regulation Finding Worksheet

Complete the worksheet before you begin researching.

Starting information: Fill in unknown information as you find it.

Regulation citation:

Regulation name:

Regulation topic/area of law:

Initial Questions

Is it state or federal?

What agency might administer this regulation?

Am I sure that I am looking for a regulation? Why?

Tracking Information: From the keywords and other information you have, plot your strategy for finding the regulation. What will be your first step and why? Complete this section of the worksheet before you actually begin the research, then record how it worked. (Do not worry if you do not take the exact number of steps listed in the worksheet—feel free to use the back of the worksheet to list more steps. If you can complete the task in fewer steps, celebrate your improved research skills!)

Step One:

Plan:

How Did It Work?

Step Two:

Plan:

How Did It Work?

Step Three:

Plan:

How Did It Work?

Step Four:

Plan:

How Did It Work?

Step Five:

Plan:

How Did It Work?

Worksheet

Regulation Research Toolbox

Use this chart to comment on the Web sites listed and to include information on your favorites.

Web site: Westlaw (**www. westlaw.com**)

Favorite Features:

Comments:

Web site: Lexis (**www.lexis.com**)

Favorite Features:

Comments:

Web site: Loislaw (**www.loislaw.com**)

Favorite Features:

Comments:

Web site: CD Law (**www.cdlaw.com**)

Favorite Features:

Comments:

Web site: FindLaw (**www.findlaw.com**)

Favorite Features:

Comments:

Web site: Legal Information Institute (**www.law.cornell.edu**)

Favorite Features:

Comments:

Web site: US Department of Agriculture (**www.usda.gov**)

Favorite Features:

Comments:

Web site:

Favorite Features:

Comments:

Web site:

Favorite Features:

Comments:

Web site:

Favorite Features:

Comments:

7

Finding Cases

Chapter Objectives

- **Review case law:** Finding cases online is quicker and easier than using the books.
- **Learn strategies for searching case law:** When searching for cases, you will learn to find cases when you have a citation, party names, or a topic.

On the Web:

- Annotated links leading you to:
  - United States Supreme Court case archives
  - State and federal cases online
- Exercises for extra help

Review of Case Law

Case law
interpretation of statutory and regulatory law by the judicial branch.

Case law is created primarily in appellate courts. You have undoubtedly studied the structure of the court system, and your understanding of it is of foremost importance when doing case research. If you are confused about the structure of the courts and the name of each level, you might be unable to make much progress in electronic case research. Indeed, you might not realize whether a case meets your needs if you do not understand where the case came from and its impact on other courts.

Check the end of the chapter for a handy chart (Table 7-3) with at least the structure of the federal courts. In Table 7-4, you can enter your state court information. With this information, you are ready to begin your electronic search for case law.

Case Law Search Strategy

Generally, when you need to look for a case, you start with at least one piece of information: a citation, party names, or a topic. The next sections look at the different research strategies that you might use.

Finding a Case with a Citation

A citation makes your search for case law quick and easy. Most electronic search tools have a place, separate from the ordinary search box, where you can simply enter the citation and find your case. This is true whether you are using Westlaw, Lexis, Loislaw or the Internet. When using Westlaw or Lexis, updating your citation on the spot is also simple. That is a great habit to get into, because far too often, legal researchers neglect the important step of updating their primary law.

Duty to Check Your Cite

Cite checking
see Shepardizing.

As a legal researcher, you have a duty to **cite check** or Shepardize, that is, to verify the validity of your citations to make sure they are still good law. Visit the Shepard's Web site (**www.shepards.com**) to see dozens of cases in which the court chastised attorneys for not checking their cites and thus missing some otherwise obvious information. Cite checking is easy to skip, but doing so can lead to embarrassment and potential liability for your firm.[1]

Bluebook
style guide with a uniform system of citation. A small book with a blue cover, bluebook is used by most legal professionals for proper citation format.

When looking for cases with the citation, you must be careful about how you enter the citation. Use basic **Bluebook** form, although you generally do not have to include periods or spacing; that will save you a few keystrokes. You do not need to enter party names, dates, or parallel citations. Do not spell out abbreviations or create your own. Make a point to check the Help section for the abbreviation protocol of the resources you choose. All of these practices help you avoid the frustration of entering a good citation but not finding any cases.

Guided Exercise

Table 7-1 lists the main sources discussed in this text and provides abbreviated formats for citations. Look up the following citations. Use at least one paid legal database and one Internet resource. Use more resources if you have access to them.

a. *Ducolon Mechanical, Inc. v. Shinstine/Forness, Inc.*, 77 Wash. App. 707, 893 P.2d 1127 (1995)
b. *Bank v Truck Ins. Exch.*, 51 F.3d 736 (7th Cir. 1995)
c. *State v Chang*, 587 N.W.2d 459 (Iowa 1997)

Parallel citation
second location for the same case. For example, a case might be found both in a state reporter and the regional reporter

You may notice that the format varies from source to source. *Note*: As a general rule of efficiency, if you have a **parallel citation**, you should enter the one with fewer characters. Usually you can enter either one of the citations to find the case. See Table 7-1 for an example of citation abbreviation styles for cases.

Table 7-1: Abbreviation format for Case law		
Source	*Format*	*Comments*
Westlaw	a. 77 wash app 707 b. 51 f3d 736 c. 587 nw 2d 459	No need to use capital letters or periods. The spacing included here is also unnecessary—you can run numbers and letters together.
Lexis	a. 77 wash app 707 b. 51 f3d 736 c. 587 nw 2d 459	No need to use capital letters or periods.
Loislaw	a. 77 wn app 707 b. 51 f3d 736 c. 587 nw2d 459	Be careful with citation format. Use strict Bluebook format.
CD Law	a. 77 wash app 707	Only WA cases are available on CD Law.
FindLaw	a. NA b. NA c. NA	Frequently, you cannot find cases in FindLaw with the average citation. You need the decision date, docket number, or party names.
Legal Information Institute	a. NA b. NA c. NA	The Cornell Law School site connects you to other Web sites. Many are not searchable by simple citation. Rather, you need the decision date, docket number, or party names.

**Exercise
7-1**

> Practice the skills you learned in this section by completing Exercise 7-1 at the end of this chapter.

Finding a Case with Party Names

Searching with party names is pretty straightforward if you are aware of a couple of things. First, depending on where and how you search, you may get back several results with the same party names. Those results might include earlier decisions in lower courts, rehearings of the same case, or denials of *certiorari* by the court of last resort. If you have information in addition to party names, like the reporter or date, quickly searching the results for that information is easy and may help you find what you want. If not, do not be afraid to actually open the cases to see if one meets your needs.

Plaintiff
person who sues at the trial court level.

Defendant
party who is being sued at the trial court level.

Here's another thing to remember when you search for party names: You do not always need to enter both names. For example, criminal cases have *State* or *People* as the **plaintiff**. That means that the government is suing on behalf of the people. Since the government files thousands of cases every year, entering *State* or *People* as the party name is not likely to enhance your results. Try just entering the **defendant's** name. For example, for the case *State v Brandemies*, just enter the party name *Brandemies*.

For common party names, like Smith or Jones, make use of any other information you have. For example, many databases let you use date restrictions. If you know the year of the decision, you can use it to limit your results. So, a party name search for the case *State v Smith* might find many cases in addition to the one you want. If you can, also include the jurisdiction, dates, and docket number to narrow the results.

The next sections include some database specific information.

Case with Party Names on Westlaw

In Westlaw, if you first select your database, you can choose the Search by Title tab and enter the party name there. There is a separate space for entering a second party name. Remember that the second party name is optional but useful, if one or both of the party names are common.

You can also perform the Find by Title function manually, using the regular search box. The abbreviation of the Find by Title function is *ti*. You can use one party name in this manner:

> ti(delahunty)

If you choose to use both party names, join them with AND, abbreviated in Westlaw with the ampersand (&). For example,

> ti(delahunty & morgan)

The Find by Title function is easy to use whether you use the tab or do it manually. It can be especially useful if you are not certain of the citation or how to abbreviate it.

Case with Party Names on Lexis

In Lexis.com, you can search by party name under the Get a Document option. Select Party Name from the three tabs under the Get A Document tab near the top of the Lexis.com screen. There are separate boxes for party names.

Using the dial-up Lexis version, you can search by party name by using the Segments option and searching for the NAME of the document. For example:

NAME(delahunty)

If you choose to use both party names, join them with AND. For example:

NAME(delahunty AND morgan)

The Segments option is especially useful if you have the party names but are not certain of the citation or how to abbreviate it.

Case with Party Names on Loislaw

In Loislaw, you need to be a bit more certain of what you are looking for. First, you must be fairly specific when selecting a database. For example, Loislaw has separate databases for state appellate and state supreme court decisions. If you do not know the court level, remember that you can select multiple databases to search. Simply select the ones that seem most likely to yield results. If the citation is from a regional reporter, the best option is to select all cases in the database. The Advanced Search option lets you enter the party names on the appellant/appellee or plaintiff/defendant line.

Another useful tool in Loislaw is the NEAR operator. Use it in the basic search box. By entering the party names, separated by the NEAR# operator (with a relatively small number like 2 or 3), you should be able to reduce the number of irrelevant results.[2] For example, you might enter the query:

Delahunty NEAR3 morgan

You will find that query an effective way to search for a party name using the basic search box.

Case with Party Names on CD Law

In CD Law and other small databases that have no specific party name search area, you can search for a party name using the appropriate Boolean search operators in the regular search box. Try joining the party names with a proximity operator like NEAR.

Case with Party Names on the Internet

You can also search by party name using the Internet. The method is quite similar to party name searches on paid legal databases. Be aware of the types of search boxes for entering the party names. If the site has a box for each name, you can enter one party name in each box. If not, you generally want to avoid entering something like *Smith v Jones* in a single search box. Instead, search using the familiar Boolean search operators, and try a query like:

Smith AND Jones or Smith NEAR Jones

Be Aware of the Date of the Case

The sample cases presented in this text are all fairly recent. That is because, with the exception of selected United States Supreme Court cases, cases decided prior to the mid 1990s are generally not on the Internet. Remember that when you have trouble finding older cases on the Internet.

Guided Exercise

Table 7-2 lists the main sources discussed in this text and provides formats for names. Look at the following citations. Using the information in Table 7-2, determine the names. Use at least one paid legal database and one Internet site.

Note how the format varies from source to source, as illustrated in Table 7-2.

   a. *People of California v Halaliku Kaloni Tufunga*, 21 Cal. 4th 935, 987 P. 2d 168 (1999)
   b. *Marshall Dominguez v. Paul Davidson*, 266 Kan. 296, 974 P.2d 112 (1999)
   c. *Carol Kolstad v American Dental Association*, 527 US 526 (1999)

See Table 7-2 for examples of how to enter case names.

Table 7-2: Abbreviation format for party names

Source	Format	Comments
Westlaw	a. Tufunga	a. With unusual party names, if you select the proper jurisdiction, you can just enter one name to find the case successfully.
	b. Dominguez (in the second line) Davidson	b. If you choose to use both party names, put the second party name in the second line provided in Find by Title.
	c. Kolstad (and optionally in the second line), ADA	c. Shorten long names with appropriate abbreviations.
Lexis	a. Tufunga	a. With unusual party names, you can just select the right jurisdiction, enter one name, and you should get the case.
	b. Dominguez AND Davidson	b. If you choose to use both party names, join them with AND.
	c. Kolstad AND ADA	c. Shorten long names with appropriate abbreviations.

(continues)

Loislaw	a. Tufunga	a. Using the California State case database, you need only one name to find the case.
	b. Dominguez & Davidson	b. Use either AND or its symbol (&) to join the party names when using more than one.
	c. Kolstad & American Dental Association	c. Using the *ADA* abbreviation yielded no results in this search. Spell long party names. However, you do not need a phrase connector to get accurate results.
FindLaw	a. Tufunga	a. Using the California State case database, only one name was needed to find the case.
	b. Dominguez Davidson	b. Using AND or v. yielded no results. Simply enter the party names.
	c. Kolstad	c. FindLaw instructions suggest entering only one party name.
Legal Information Institute	a. Tufunga	a. Simply entering this unique party name in the search box yielded an accurate result as the second hit.
	b. Dominguez (and in the second line) Davidson	b. Select the highest court when you are uncertain of the jurisdiction. Use Advanced Search whenever you can. Using it here allowed for a title (party name) search.
	c. Kolstad	c. Entering this unique party name in the Quick Search box of the Supreme Court Collection brought the desired case as the first hit.

Exercise 7-2

Practice the skills you learned in this section by completing Exercise 7-2 at the end of the chapter.

Finding a Case with a Topic

Searching for case law electronically with a topic is much like doing any other topic search. It may help to recall the Boolean search strategies and the Five Questions described earlier in this text.

The main difference between general topic searches and searching for cases by topic is the database you select. Focusing on the appropriate case database puts you on the right track.

Searching by name and citation produces fairly limited results. However, topic searching is likely to provide dozens if not hundreds of results.

Case with Topic on Westlaw and Lexis

If your Westlaw or Lexis search finds too many documents, you can narrow your results using the Westlaw Locate tool or the Lexis Focus tool. Those tools enable you to search the results of your current search. This is a great help if your initial search is on the right track but yields too many results to work with efficiently.

This text regularly advocates searching the narrowest possible database. The Locate and Focus tools let you search the relatively small database of your current search results, so you can pinpoint your results even more. See the Lexis and Westlaw manuals for more information on how the tools work.

Case with Topic on Loislaw and CD Law

In databases like Loislaw and CD Law, you can do topic searches using the regular search box with the appropriate Boolean search operators. Several basic strategies that work in Lexis and Westlaw work in these databases as well. If needed, narrow your search using the narrowest possible database and additional keywords.

Case with Topic on the Internet

When you do a topic case search on the Internet, the same tools you used in earlier chapters serve you well. You need to select an appropriate place to do your search. The same sites mentioned earlier, including Findlaw and the Legal Information Institute, are useful here as well. Take a moment to check how far back the cases on that Web site date before conducting your search. Also take a moment to look at the search criterion to make sure your query will be effective.

Exercises 7-3 and 7-4

Practice the skills you learned in this section by completing Exercises 7-3 and 7-4 at the end of this chapter.

SUMMARY

Whether you have a citation, party names, a topic, or a combination of these, finding a case is a fairly straightforward task. You can search effectively using any of the electronic resources discussed in this chapter. Remember this one limitation: Cases on the Internet tend to be more recent. However, most Web sites tell you the date range of cases on the search screen, so you can easily learn what is available.

The ease of searching for cases is fortunate, since cases are also a great way to find statutes and regulations, as discussed in Chapters 5 and 6. You might find that case law research is the type of research you do most.

Notes

1. See "Duty to Shepardize" on Shepard's Help Cite page
   http://helpcite.shepards.com/
2. For more helpful research tips, look at the Help section of Loislaw. It includes a very user-friendly section on how to use Boolean search operators to search Loislaw effectively.

EXERCISES

Exercise 7-1

Find the names of the following cases, and answer the related question. Use one or more search tools so you can compare results. (*Hint*: Generally, you do not need to read the entire case to complete these exercises. Use the headnotes or other summaries to find the answers.)

1. Was the applicant denied due process? 57 F.Supp.2d. 1305 (1999)

2. Whose duty is it to engage in prosecutorial discretion? 127 N.M. 566, 985 P.2d 168 (1999)

3. Under Minnesota law, how should contractual provisions be interpreted? 186 F.3d 981 (1999)

4. What does a plaintiff have to demonstrate to get a preliminary injunction? 673 N.Y.S.2d 450, 242 A.D.2d 52 (1998)

5. What is the precise and universal test of relevancy? 48 Conn. App. 717, 711 A.2d 769 (1998)

6. When should the *per se* rule be applied? 143 F.3d 914 (1998)

Exercise 7-2

Use the party name and jurisdictional information below to answer the following questions. Include the full citations in your answers. Try using a variety of resources to answer the questions.

1. What is the four-part test for determining whether injunctive relief should be granted? *Doe v. Fauver* (D.N.J. 1997)

2. What impact do "fighting words" have? *Lundgren v. State* (Ga. App. 1999)

3. If it looks like a criminal defendant might be insane, who in Massachusetts bears the burden of disproving that? *Commonwealth v. Federici* (Mass 1998)

4. What does this Michigan court think about expert testimony regarding the credibility of a witness? *Franzel v. Kerr Manufacturing Company* (Mich. App. 1999)

5. When is extrinsic evidence admissible to determine the grantors intent in an easement? *Perillo v. Credendino* (N.Y.A.D. 2 Dept 1999)

6. When should expert testimony be excluded? *Bryant v. Buerman* (Fla. App. 4 Dist 1999)

Exercise 7-3

Use case law to answer the following questions. There is not necessarily one right answer for each. Just try to find a case that accurately answers each question. Try using a variety of resources to answer the questions. (You might recall these questions from Chapter 1.)

1. Did Dick slander Jane when he wrote and published a truthful editorial about her bad housekeeping?

2. Is Lars liable for fraud because he sold stock for a company that did not exist?

3. Did Henry breach his contract with Luis when Henry delivered fresh flowers a day late and when time was of the essence?

4. Did Zora make a valid will when she left her entire estate to her cat, Mr. Pipo?

5. Is Badco liable for discrimination when it refuses to hire female workers over age of 24?

Chapter Review Exercises

Answer the questions below using the information provided. Try to use at least two different search tools, and compare their effectiveness. Comparisons can help you expand your research toolbox, enabling you to research more effectively in the future.

1. Bang's cat regularly enters Bing's yard to use the garden as a litter box. Can Bing sue Bang for the tort of trespass?

2. What is the general legal subject covered in the case located at 900 P.2d 113 (1995)?

3. Can Melody sue Off Note Records for using her copywrited song without her permission?

4. What elements are needed to show intentional infliction of emotional distress?

5. What type of damages did Lord's and Lady's Enterprises, Inc. get in their 1999 case heard in the Massachusetts Appeals Court?

6. Deneen Sweeting was a defendant in the third circuit in 2000. What aspect of criminal law is his case about?

Table 7-3

Name of Court	Court Level	Case Reporter	Abbreviation
Federal District Court	Trial Court	Federal Supplement	F. Supp.
United States Court of Appeals	Appellate Court	Federal Reporter	F., F.2d, F.3d
United States Supreme Court	Appellate Court of last resort	United States Reports Supreme Court Reporter Lawyer's Edition	U.S. S.Ct. L.Ed.

Now, fill in the same information for the courts in your state.

Table 7-4

Name of Court	Court Level	Case Reporter	Abbreviation

Worksheet

New Database Worksheet

Use this worksheet to record the relevant search information you discover when you explore new databases.

Database:

Boolean Search:

Proximity Search:

Phrase Search:

Stemming:

Wildcard:

Worksheet

Case Research Toolbox

Use this chart to comment on the Web sites listed and to include information on your favorites.

Website: Westlaw (**www.westlaw.com**)

Favorite Features:

Comments:

Website: Lexis (**www.lexis.com**)

Favorite Features:

Comments:

Website: Loislaw (**www.loislaw.com**)

Favorite Features:

Comments:

Website: CD Law (**www.cdlaw.com**)

Favorite Features:

Comments:

Website: FindLaw (**www.findlaw.com**)

Favorite Features:

Comments:

Website: Legal Information Institute (**www.law.cornell.edu**)

Favorite Features:

Comments:

Web site:

Favorite Features:

Comments:

Web site:

Favorite Features:

Comments:

Web site:

Favorite Features:

Comments:

Web site:

Favorite Features:

Comments:

8

Finding Secondary Sources

Chapter Objectives

- **Use dictionaries and encyclopedias:** Students generally reserve dictionaries and encyclopedias for topics they know nothing about, or they ignore these valuable sources altogether. You'll learn the several good reasons to start every research project with these sources.

- **Include law review articles:** Almost every topic you can imagine has been researched before. You can avoid reinventing the wheel by including law review articles in your research process.

- **Explore practice books, hornbooks, restatements, and other explanatory material:** These sources generally go into great depth, clearly and concisely explaining every element of the topics they cover.

- **Research legal and other news:** Legal newspapers, periodicals, and other news sources are valuable research tools.

On the Web:

- Annotated links leading you to:
  - Web resources for each category listed as a chapter objective
- Exercises for additional help

Introduction

Law librarians have a valuable research secret: Start with **secondary sources**. As most legal professionals agree, starting your research with secondary sources serves several functions.

- **You can focus on the right keywords.** Beginning your research with a secondary source like a legal encyclopedia, a legal dictionary, or words and phrases gives you a firm idea of relevant topics and leads you to appropriate legal keywords. Often, you might choose words that are not those used in cases and statutes. Starting with secondary sources helps to point you in the right direction.

- **You can avoid reinventing the wheel.** Hundreds of **law review articles**, **ALRs** (American Law Reports), and other sources of legal writing contain information based on in-depth research on a number of subjects. Most likely, the issue you are researching has been researched before. When you find an article on point, it generally includes an overview of the topic followed by a careful analysis of the intricacies of one portion of the subject. Hundreds of relevant cases, statutes, and additional secondary sources support this analysis, bringing you closer to your research goals.

- **You can deepen your perspective.** Frequently, when you begin research-ing, you already have a good understanding of the topic. You have an idea of where you want to go and how to focus your research appropriately. This is great, but it is possible that in narrowing your search at the outset, you eliminate other important areas to research. Reading secondary sources on your research topic helps you see the topic versus true depth and makes your end result more useful to the attorney and the client.

In addition to providing background information on a topic, one main purpose of secondary sources is to lead the researcher to primary sources. Back in the "old days" (mid-1990s) when most research was done by book, a researcher was almost forced to use secondary sources because finding the primary sources without them was so much harder. With electronic legal research tools avail-able, that heavy reliance on secondary sources to lead you to primary sources is dwindling. It is simple to do a keyword search of the texts of statutes and cases and to stumble around in that fashion until you find something. However, the ease of finding primary sources online takes away none of the great reasons listed above for beginning your research with secondary sources. The use of secondary sources is a sound strategy used by professionals and is one you should adopt as well.

**Overcoming
Research
Hurdles**

Many students who run into trouble researching start their research in the wrong place. When asked where they began, they usually respond by naming the cases or statutes that they are trying, in vain, to search for. When asked why they started there, they usually have no answer. When you run into a block in your research, ask yourself where you began and why you started there. If you have no good answer, return to the Five Questions (Chapter 2) and use them to refocus. If all else fails, do not be afraid to ask an instructor or librarian for help.

Now you know all the benefits of using secondary sources. The next sections look at their electronic availability.

Dictionaries and Encyclopedias

Legal dictionary
resource for word definitions. Specific legal dictionaries are an excellent starting point for research.

Legal dictionaries and **legal encyclopedias** are great places to start because both help you to focus your keywords and both help to lay a foundation for later research. Many are readily available online.

Westlaw Dictionaries and Encyclopedias

Legal encyclopedia
secondary source with brief explanations of legal terms and concepts, often accompanied by references to relevant cases.

Westlaw makes some major secondary sources available on its databases. *Black's Law Dictionary* (abbreviated in Westlaw as DI)[1] and the legal encyclopedia *American Jurisprudence* (AMJUR) are great places to start.

Lexis Dictionaries and Encyclopedias

Lexis also offers some major secondary sources in its Lexis Reference collection (abbreviated in Lexis as LEXREF). *Ballentine's Law Dictionary* (BTINES) and the legal encyclopedia *American Jurisprudence* (AMJUR) are great places to start.

Loislaw and CD Law

Neither Loislaw nor CD Law provides much in the way of secondary sources, and neither has legal dictionaries or encyclopedias.

The Internet's Dictionaries and Encyclopedias

The Internet is itself a secondary source. Web pages frequently give you background information and lead you to primary sources. So, you can utilize your basic Internet search skills to find secondary information on the Internet. Give yourself an edge by starting your search in a legal directory like FindLaw (**www.findlaw.com**) or the Law Engine (**www.thelawengine.com**). They make it easy to identify and browse through various categories of secondary sources. In addition, you can go to a legal directory, and find a reference section that lists a variety of legal dictionaries available on the Web.

Guided Exercise

As mentioned, you can use the Internet as one giant secondary source. Suppose you need to find out whether the statute of limitations has run on a particular case. You decide to start at the beginning—with the definition of the statute of limitations.

1. **Go to a legal dictionary online.** Find the definition of the *statute of limitations*. Visit FindLaw (**www.findlaw.com**). The search box gives you a variety of choices. The default is FindLaw Guide, but if you use the dropdown menu, you will see that you can use that search box to search a legal dictionary.

2. **Enter the search term in the search box.** Read the entire definition. Does it make sense to you? Even if you know what a statute of limitations is, you might find the Findlaw's definition a little complicated.

3. **Try to find a simpler definition.** Nolo.com (**www.nolo.com**) is a useful legal encyclopedia, and a great addition to your set of Web sites that you regularly refer to in your research, your toolbox of favorites. Knowing which specific sites to visit for additional information saves you a lot of time. The Nolo Web site provides additional clarification on the statute of limitations. Its plain language definition might not be the wording you would use in a legal document, however, it might be very helpful in constructing a more effective search. The drawback of sites like Nolo is that they only cover basic issues of interest to the lay person.

Exercise 8-1	Practice the skills you learned in this section by completing Exercise 8-1, at the end of this chapter. Remember to use the Web sites you put in your Internet toolbox.

Law Review Articles

You can take advantage of others' research by searching for and reading law review articles.

Law Review Articles on Westlaw

Bar journal
legal periodical aimed at the practicing attorney.

Hundreds of legal periodicals are available in Westlaw's Law Reviews, Bar Journals, and Legal Periodicals database, from the *American Bar Association Journal* (ABAJ) to the *Yale Law and Policy Review* (YLLPR). You are probably familiar with law reviews, but you may be less familiar with **bar journals**. Bar journals differ from law reviews in one basic way: bar journals are geared toward practicing attorneys who deal with the everyday problems of running or working in a law office. Because of that, fewer bar journal articles discuss theoretical and academic approaches to the law. Rather, the articles focus on practical application of the law. You can also find very current practice topics in bar journal articles.

Westlaw gives you three ways to find specific articles on your topic. First, if you have a citation, you can go to Find A Document to find your article. This is, as always, the easiest way to find a document. You can also search generally, using keywords to search the combined law review and bar journal database (JLR) or to perform a broader search of Major Secondary Publications (MAJSECPUBS). In the Law Review, Bar Journals, and Legal Periodicals database, you can also find *American Law Reports* (ALR), *Corpus Juris Secundum* (CJS) Restatements, *Uniform Laws*,[2] and other legal texts.

The third way to search law review articles using Westlaw is through some sort of topic grouping. You can search the law reviews of your state. (Use the two-letter state abbreviation plus JLR, for example, CA-JLR or WY-JLR.) Or, you can do a topic search. Westlaw lets you search by practice area in the Topical Materials by Area of Practice database. From there, you can find combined legal periodicals under topics like Education (ED-TP), Maritime Law (MRT-TP), or Taxation (TX-TP).

If you have no ideas about the topic, try using dictionaries or encyclopedia to find some relevant information. Narrowing your search to a topic search rather than searching the broader combined law review databases generally yields more targeted results.

Law Review Articles on Lexis

Lexis has over 200 law review databases available in its Law Reviews Library (LAWREV). It also includes a good selection of bar journals. Bar journals differ from law reviews in one basic way. Bar journals' audience is practicing attorneys who are involved daily in the problems of running or working in a law office. Therefore, only a minority of articles deal with the theoretical and academic aspects of law. The majority discuss its practical application. Most bar journal articles also focus on very current practice topics.

In Lexis, use Lexsee to look up law review articles by citation. You can also search generally, using keywords to search the combined law review files (ALLREV) or the combined law journal files (BARJNL). You can also get *American Law Reports* (ALR) in the Law Reviews Library, and search the combined ALR and law reviews databases as well (LRALR).

Topic grouping is another way to search law review articles on Lexis. You can search the law reviews of your state using the two-letter state abbreviation plus LRV, for example, CALRV or NYLRV. You can also search by topic. Topics include Corporate Law (CORPLR), Family Law (FAMLR), Intellectual Property Law (IPLR), and Tax Law (TAXLR).

If you are completely unfamiliar with the topic, try to find some guidance in dictionaries or encyclopedias. You will generally get better results by narrowing your search to a topic database rather than searching the combined law review databases.

Loislaw and CD Law

Again, Loislaw and CD Law do not generally contain many secondary materials. At their libraries contain no law reviews.

A Note on Citations

As a general rule, you do not cite secondary sources in formal legal documents like court pleadings. Citing secondary sources is perfectly fine in informal legal memoranda and other informal documents. Remember that, in addition to helping you find background information, secondary sources' purpose is to lead you to primary sources of law. In formal legal documents, cite the primary sources that the secondary sources lead you to, rather than the secondary sources themselves.

Law Review Articles on the Internet

More and more law review articles are available on the Internet. You can find them in two ways. If you are interested in a specific law review journal, you can go directly to its Web site. For example, you might want to find an article in the *Cardozo Law Review*. Do a phrase search in your favorite search engine to get its address (**http://www.cardozo.yu.edu/cardlrev/index.html**). Alternatively, you can visit a Web page that lists a variety of law journals and browse until you find what you want. The USC Legal Journals page (**http://www.usc.edu/dept/law-lib/legal/journals.html**) is a great resource that lets you know which journals have the full text of articles online, as opposed to abstracts or tables of contents. The drawback of journals on the Internet is inconvenience. Using Westlaw or Lexis, you can do a keyword search through hundreds of legal journals at the same time. Using the Internet, you must search the journals one at a time.

Exercise 8-2

Practice your skills at finding law journal articles by completing Exercise 8-2 at this end of this chapter.

Practice books, Hornbooks, Restatements, and Other Explanatory Material

These sources provide very detailed information in a clear concise manner.

Explanatory Sources on Westlaw

Westlaw libraries have a great selection of valuable secondary sources. You can access the information in a few ways. If you know that a specific secondary source exists, you can search to find the publication and then do a keyword search of that source only. To search the list of publications, open Find a Document and click Publications. In Westlaw.com, you can find the same information by clicking Find a Database.

If you do not have the name of a specific publication, you can browse the Topical materials by Area of Practice. That leads you to the categories and names of individual secondary sources to search. Imagine you are looking for information on torts. If so, you might find the *Andrews Mass Tort Litigation Reporter* or *Punitive Damages: A State-by-State Guide to Law and Practice*. You can search these sources independently or in a combined search of tort-related periodicals, texts, and journals (TRT-TP).

A third alternative is to do a global search of all texts and periodicals combined (TP-ALL), using a selection of keywords. This is a good choice if you are not entirely sure of the topic or if you would like to broaden your research horizon.

Explanatory Sources on Lexis

Lexis has a variety of **practice books, hornbooks**, and **restatements**. There are a few ways to access that information. If you know that a specific secondary source exists, you can search for and to find the publication and then search only that source for keywords.

If you do not know a specific publication's name, you can browse the Areas of Law by Topic library. That leads you to the names of categories or individual secondary sources to search. Suppose you want information on torts. If so, you might find the *BNA Toxics Law Daily* (BNATLD).

Another alternative is to globally search a combination of secondary sources using a selection of keywords. This approach is good if you are not entirely sure of the topic or if you want to broaden your research.

Practice book

legal reference aimed at the practicing attorney. Often in a three-ring binder, the practice book is meant to be a current reference on everything relevant to its specific subject area.

Hornbook

textbook-like, in-depth, and detailed exploration of a broad legal topic like torts or contracts.

Restatement

textbook-like exploration of a single legal subject for which most law is developed in the courts.

Read What You Cite

When you find a secondary source with a wealth of cases on point, relying on the analysis that you find there is tempting. And so is including that analysis in your research results. After all, the authors are the experts, and you do not want to reinvent the wheel. You must avoid the temptation to adopt the professional's analysis as your own. You need to read the primary sources so you can draw your own conclusions as they relate to your unique set of facts. You should read every case or statute that you cite in your final document. And don't forget to Shepardize!

Explanatory Services on Loislaw and CD Law

Loislaw has a limited selection of state continuing legal education (CLE) materials. CLE materials are aimed at the practicing attorney and, like the practice book, present useful information about the law as it is practiced in the field. Although CLE, materials are not available for every state, you may find looking at another state's materials useful in developing your research.

CD Law currently contains no secondary sources.

Explanatory Services on the Internet

The Internet is also a weak option for finding hornbooks and practice books online. This is because these books tend to be privately published and thus are not freely available on the Internet. You may find that the information is available on the Internet for a small fee, but if you have Westlaw or Lexis, they are a better bet.

Legal and Other News

The many legal newspapers, periodicals, and other news sources available on-line are valuable for research.

News Sources on Westlaw

Westlaw's selection of legal news sources is bound to help you find the information you need. You can search the Combined News Databases in general (ALLNEWS) or state-by-state (using the two-letter state abbreviation plus NEWS, for example, HI-NEWS or FL-NEWS). General interest magazines, newsletters, and television transcripts of programs like *60 Minutes* (60MIN) are also available. Collections include both national and international holdings.

News Sources on Lexis

The Lexis Legal News Library (LEGNEW) permits you to search news made in the last two years (CURNWS), older news (ACRNWS), or a combination of both (ALLNWS). Legal newsletters on specific areas of law are also available, including "Entertainment Law" (ENTLTR), "Intellectual Property" (IPLTR), and "Computer Law" (COMPTR). Collections include both national and international holdings.

News Sources on Loislaw, CD Law, and the Internet

While neither Loislaw nor CD Law carries much legal news, several Web sites provide excellent legal news and analysis. Many major news outlets, like the *New York Times* (**www.nytimes.com**), have special sections on legal news. FindLaw also has a special news site (**news.findlaw.com**) that sends legal news updates by e-mail on a daily basis. Indeed, many news providers, including Westlaw and Lexis, provide legal news by e-mail. This is an excellent and relatively painless way to stay on top of the subjects most important to you or your client.

SUMMARY

Secondary sources have been and will continue to be an excellent way to begin legal research. They lead you to key cases; they give you expert, in-depth analysis; and they help you to focus your search. Secondary sources also assist you by adding depth and perspective, especially when you do not know the subject matter very well. Secondary sources are simple to access and provide a wealth of information. Do not neglect this most important step of legal research.

Notes

1. Source abbreviations are included here because it is often easier to search for secondary sources by abbreviation than it is to browse for them.
2. Remember, uniform laws are secondary sources until they are adopted by individual states. At that point, the states adopted version of the secondary source becomes the primary source.

EXERCISES

Exercise 8-1

Answer the following questions using an electronic legal dictionary or encyclopedia. You can use Lexis, Westlaw, or the Internet. Support your answers by citing your sources.

1. What is *proximate cause* as it relates to the tort of negligence?

2. When does a party to a contract have to *cover*?

3. What elements are necessary to establish joint tenancy?

4. What is an example of *res ipsa loquitor*?

5. What is a *corporate veil*?

6. What is the basis of *in rem* jurisdiction?

Exercise 8-2

Now that you know the meaning of the terms in exercise 8-1, find a law review article that describes each in more detail. Again, you can use Lexis, Westlaw, or the Internet. Try using a combination of resources so that you can further develop your skills. Support your answers by citing your sources. Note the subtle ways in which your queries change when you look for the same information in different places.

Chapter Review Exercises

Find answers to the following questions using secondary sources. Note the secondary sources in which you find your answers. The words in italics give you great places to start.

1. Josie worked as a maid for Happy Housecleaners. She enjoyed her job, especially since she got to view beautiful things every day in the houses she visited. However, the more beautiful things that Josie saw, the more she wanted them for herself. One day, while cleaning the home of the wealthy Mrs. Miser, Josie saw a lovely figurine of a woman with her cat. She just had to have it. The small figurine was on a shelf with dozens of other figurines. Josie doubted Mrs. Miser would miss it. She slipped the figurine into her pocket and took it home, where she gave it a place of honor on her mantle.

   Two days later, the police came for Josie and charged her with theft. Mrs. Miser also wanted to sue Happy Housecleaners for damages under the theory of *respondeat superior*, since Josie was their employee. Can Mrs. Miser sue under the theory?

2. The elderly yet spry Magdelina Esperanza Guapa lived in a small house that she had inherited as a *life estate* from her mother. After Magdelina's death, the house was to go to her niece Estrella. Magdelina did not like Estrella, as the girl tended to be flighty and got engaged to a different young man every few months. So, Magdelina sold the small house to her gardener, Jorge, for a bargain price, hoping that Estrella would never get the house. Magdelina moved to a retirement condominium where she had an active social life until she died three years later.

   Two weeks after Magdelina's funeral, Estrella went to the little house and demanded that Jorge surrender it to her. Does Jorge have any rights here, or does he have to surrender the house to Estrella?

3. Skipper was selling her boat, the Malibu, for $50,000. Kev saw the boat and really wanted to buy it, but he had to ask his wife first. Kev offered Skipper $200 to hold the offer open to him for two days. Skipper agreed to the *firm offer* proposal. The next day, another buyer came along and offered $55,000. Skipper knew this was much more than Kev could offer, so she accepted and sold the boat to the other buyer.

Kev came back two days later with his wife's permission. He was devastated when Skipper gave him the $200 back, saying she had already sold the boat. Kev wonders whether he has any recourse against Skipper for breaching their agreement. Does he?

Worksheet

Secondary Source Research Toolbox

Use this chart to comment on the Web sites listed and to include information on your favorites.

Website: Westlaw (**www.westlaw.com**)

Favorite Features:

Comments:

Website: Lexis (**www.lexis.com**)

Favorite Features:

Comments:

Website: Loislaw (**www.loislaw.com**)

Favorite Features:

Comments:

Website: CD Law (**www.cdlaw.com**)

Favorite Features:

Comments:

Website: Findlaw **(www.findlaw.com)**

Favorite Features:

Comments:

Website: Legal Engine (**www.legalengine.com**)

Favorite Features:

Comments:

Website: Nolo (**www.nolo.com**)

Favorite Features:

Comments:

Website: Cardozo Law Review (**http://www.cardozo.yu.edu/cardlrev/index.html**)

Favorite Features:

Comments:

Website: USC Journals (**http://www.usc.edu/dept/ law-lib/legal/journals.html**)

Favorite Features:

Comments:

Website: NY Times **(www.nytimes.com)**

Favorite Features:

Comments:

Web site:

Favorite Features:

Comments:

Web site:

Favorite Features:

Comments:

Web site:

Favorite Features:

Comments:

Web site:

Favorite Features:

Comments:

Web site:

Favorite Features:

Comments:

Web site:

Favorite Features:

Comments:

Worksheet

New Database Worksheet

Use this worksheet to record the relevant search information you discover when you explore new databases.

Database:

Boolean Search:

Proximity Search:

Phrase Search:

Stemming:

Wildcard:

Legislative History

Overview of Legislative History

Your legal research text should have a section on legislative history and the tools available to perform it. Here is a quick review to help you understand the tools available to simplify your research. Keep in mind that the tools available for doing federal legislative history are likely to differ from those available for state legislative history.

Federal Legislative History

The best way to understand the process of researching legislative history is to understand the legislative process.

First, the proposed bill is introduced in either the Senate or the House of Representatives. At this point, the bill is a numbered and sent to a Congressional committee for review. It may be amended, rewritten altogether, or not acted on at all—the bill dies in committee. You can look at the *Congressional Index* for information on active bills, which includes bills in committee. Published every week while Congress is in session, it chronologically lists all bills being considered and includes basic information about their status. For information on bills in committee, you may also turn to the *United States Code, Congressional and Administrative News (USCCAN)*. This valuable resource contains the full text of selected committee reports and useful citations to related documents in the *Congressional Record*.

The committee may hold hearings on the proposed bill. The *Congressional Information Service's (CIS) Index and Abstract* contains information on congressional hearings. The index includes the publications of over 300 Congressional committees.

After the committee acts on the bill, it reports back to the Senate or the House for debate and, potentially, a vote on the bill. The *Congressional Record* reports the full text of debates in both the House and the Senate. If the body votes on and passes the bill, the entire process repeats in the next Congressional body.

Bills passed by both the House and the Senate make it to the President's desk. The President can either sign or veto the bill. The *Weekly Compilation of Presidential Documents* includes veto messages.

By looking at these publications, a researcher can do two things. First, you can follow an active bill as it goes through the process of becoming law. This is known as **bill tracking**. Second, you can look at the same process from an historical perspective and determine, from debates, reports, and the like, what the drafters meant to accomplish when they wrote the law. This is **legislative history**.

Bill tracking
following the progress of legislation as it moves from its original proposal through committees to potential passing and signing by the executive.

State Legislative History

Each of the fifty states has a law-making process similar to that of the federal government. Of course, each state has different legislative structures and publishes relevant information in different publications. The Web page associated with this text contains links that explain how to do legislative history in nearly every state in the Union.

Legislative History Resources

To research and learn about legislative history, you can refer to the many electronic sources described in this text. They include Westlaw, and Lexis, as well as state-specific sources like CD Law and the Internet.

Legislative History on Westlaw

Westlaw's database of Federal Statutes, Legislative History and Bill Tracking lets you access federal legislative history easily. Federal resources include the *Congressional Record* (CR), *Congressional Testimony* (CONGTMY or USTESTIMONY), and *Congressional Quarterly's Washington Alert* for bill tracking (CQ-BILLTRK) and its full text of bills (CQ-BILLTXT). This database also has a compilation of legislative histories from Arnold & Porter. In addition, you can find legislative histories under its individual topic areas. For example, in the Finance and Banking database, you can find Arnold & Porter's *Riegle History of the Community Development and Regulatory Improvement Act of 1994* (RIEGLE94-LH).

For state legislative history and bill tracking, Westlaw facilitates bill tracking (example: NY-BILLTRK) and viewing the full text of bills (example: NY-BILLTXT) for all fifty states. For researching older legislation, Westlaw 's Historical Legislative Service covers each state and laws dating back to the early 1990s. You can find these resources in the Statute and Court Rules directory for each state.

This is just a sample of materials available for researching legislative history on Westlaw. To see all that is available, view the Westlaw Directory for each state and the federal government.

Legislative History on Lexis

The Legislation Library (LEGIS) on Lexis includes information for researching both state and federal legislation. Federal resources include the *Congressional Record* (RECORD), full text of bills (BILLS), Senate (SENATE) and House (HOUSE) debates, and the *Daily Digest* (DIGEST). Lexis has also compiled and organized legislative histories by topic—for example, the compiled bankruptcy legislative histories (BKRLH)—and by specific act—for example, the legislative history of the Toxic Substances Control Act (TSCALH). The Legislation Library also includes news sources, Bureau of National Affairs (BNA) daily reports on a variety of topics, and a host of other resources.

For state legislative history and bill tracking, Lexis provides the full text of current and past bills for all fifty states. It also has current bill-tracking information and bill-tracking archives that contain material dating back to 1990.

This is just a sample of the materials available for researching legislative history on Lexis. Accessing a list of the full collection of materials in the Legislation Library is easy. On Lexis.com, click Legislation and Politics, then click U.S. Congress. On the dial-up version of Lexis, the library files are visible through the Classic view of Lexis.

Legislative History on CD Law

Focusing on the law of Washington State, CD Law has several resources for researching local legislative history and tracking bills. Under its Washington Legislative Materials, CD Law has legislative materials from 1995 to present, including every version of every bill introduced in the state. House and Senate reports are also included. CD Law also has *the Washington State Register*. Similar to the *Federal Register*, this publication includes proposed and final rules and publications of the governor.

Legislative History on Loislaw

Focused on state materials, Loislaw currently has no resources for researching federal or state legislative history or tracking bills.

Legislative History on the Internet

The Internet is an excellent resource for bill tracking, checking recent legislative history, and finding compiled legislative histories of popular topics.

Thomas (**http://thomas.loc.gov/**) is the major resource for current congressional information. Published by the Library of Congress, Thomas divides the information from USSCAN into sections: Legislation, Congressional Record, and Committee Information. The Legislation section includes bill summaries and a public law index that dates back as far as 1974. Full texts of bills are available dating back to 1990. The *Congressional Record* has the full text dating back to 1989, and the *Congressional Index* dates back to 1994. The

Committee Information section has committee reports dating back to the 104th Congress (1995–1996), as well as links to committee Web pages. Special sections track bills on the House floor this week and bills on the House floor now. All around, this is an excellent site.

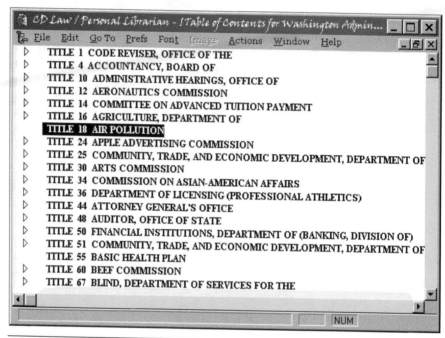

Figure A-1: Thomas Web site

You can also go directly to the source. Both the House (**www.house.gov**) and the Senate (**www.senate.gov**) have quick links from their main pages to an index of committees. A visit to the Web page of the Senate Banking Committee (**www.senate.gov/~banking/**) is illustrative. There, the researcher can find hearing information, the full text of committee reports, and links to other information relevant to committee activities.

Another way to find information about legislation is by visiting the Web sites of interested parties. For example, the American Civil Liberties Union (**www.aclu.org**) has an in-depth Web site that includes information on all issues of interest to the ACLU. The ACLU's main page has an Issues index that includes everything from Criminal Justice to Workplace Rights. Under each topic are documents and news briefs on breaking issues, as well as historical documents on the topic.

The American Association of Retired Persons (**www.aarp.org**) is another example of an interest group that provides easy to access to information on topics important to its members. From its main page, visitors can access the

Legislative Issues link to review issues regarding health, housing, and economic security. This site also includes summaries of AARP testimony to Congress.

For information on state resources, try the Web pages of the state law library or local law school law libraries. They frequently have information on the process of state legislative history and links to any available online resources.

Legislative History Search Strategy

One of the toughest parts of researching legislative history is figuring out where to start. This Legislative History Search Strategy should eliminate that problem by guiding you through the early steps of legislative history research.

Step 1: Determine why you are doing the research

Before you begin any research, you should clearly understand why you are doing the research. That might mean forming an issue question or figuring out the meaning of a word. Why are you doing this legislative history? Sometimes you just need a general history of a bill, with no particular issue. More often than not, however, you hope the history clarifies some issue or explains some term. With a clear idea of the issue or your reason for researching legislative history, you can make an intelligent decision on how to proceed. That may mean that you do not need to follow all the steps in this process, or it may mean that you need to take several more steps to find your answer.

Step 2: Get a copy of the statute

Having an actual copy of the statute helps you determine several things:

- What is the bill number?
- What year did the bill pass?
- Has the law been amended? When?

The information that you need is generally at the end of a statute. Here is an example of a federal statute, the Public Hearings section of the Coastal Zone Management Act.

16 USCS § 1457 (2000)

§ 1457. Public hearings

All public hearings required under this title must be announced at least thirty days prior to the hearing date. At the time of the announcement, all agency materials pertinent to the hearings, including documents, studies, and other data, must be made available to the public for review and study. As similar materials are subsequently developed, they shall be made available to the public as they become available to the agency.

HISTORY: (June 17, 1966, P.L. 89-454, Title III, § 311 [308], as added Oct. 27, 1972, P.L. 92-583, 86 Stat. 1287; July 26, 1976, P.L. 94-370, § 7, 90 Stat. 1019.)

The history section at the end of a statute has a plethora of useful information. First, the law in our example was proposed as Public Law (P.L.) 89-454 and signed into law on June 17, 1966. This section of the Act was amended in October of 1972 and again in 1976, as Public Law 94-370. With this information, you can easily use the resources mentioned. Keep in mind that, during the process of becoming a law, the bill is not yet codified—in other words, it has not been placed in the United States Code with a handy number like 16 USC 1457. Rather, during the consideration stage, laws are referred to by their Public Law number. As you can see, researching legislative history would be impossible without it.

The information at the end of a statute also arms you with the information needed to do some comparative research. Is your research issue current, or did the matter arise some time ago? Did the law read differently at that time? Does the current or the former law apply to your issue? Are the changes in the law's language relevant to your issue? The answers to those questions, if relevant to your issue, may lead you to important information.

Historical Research

When doing research electronically, you are generally guaranteed the most up-to-date version of the law. That is wonderful—if the most current version of the law is what you want. Often, when researching legislative history, you are interested in reading older versions of the law. To find out if there are old versions, look to the current version of the law for the original passage date and the dates of any amendments.

You can find old versions of the law in hard copy in the libraries of larger law schools or the law library associated with your state capitol. Both Westlaw and Lexis have selected archive versions of statutes at both the state and federal level.

Generally the same type of information follows state statutes as follows federal statutes. If you are uncertain what the abbreviations at the end mean, now may be a good time to actually open a book (abbreviations are always defined in the first few pages) or pick up the phone and call a local law librarian. Sometimes electronic researchers feel boxed in by their computers and forget that other resources are available. Remember that the telephone is also a great research tool. You generally have a variety of resources available to you. The skillful researcher knows how and when to use them all.

Step 3: Does a legislative history already exist for this bill?

Often the information in compiled legislative histories is all you need to answer your question. For federal law, check *USCCAN, Congressional Information*

Services, and the *Congressional Record.* They often have citations to existing legislative histories. Also, the annotated version of a statute may have information about existing histories or detailed law review articles that include a historical perspective. Both Westlaw and Lexis have sections with existing legislative histories that you can easily search. Existing legislative histories can save you lots of work. People who are experts in their respective fields created most of the compiled legislative histories. Thus, a compiled legislative history can give you a more global perspective, which may be hard to obtain if you are not already intimately familiar with the subject matter that the statute addresses.

Step 4: What other specific information do I need?

Steps 1 through 4 should give you a general legislative history and answer many of your questions about the legislation. If you need to answer a more specific question, however, those steps may not be enough, especially if you cannot find an existing legislative history. If that is the case, you may need to begin to compile your own legislative history, using the materials noted here. Refer to your legal research text for more information on compiling legislative histories.

B

Regulatory Guidance and Rule Tracking

Introduction

Regulatory guidance is the regulatory version of legislative history. Regulatory interpretation or guidance is information from an agency about how it intends to interpret its law. That "straight-from-the-horse's mouth" information can be invaluable for the regulated community because it greatly reduces the guesswork of trying to figure out what regulations really mean. Although a regulation's purpose is to clarify statutes written by Congress or the legislature, sometimes the clarification needs clarifying. That's where the guidance comes in.

Review of the Rule-making Process

Before a bill becomes a law, several steps must be completed. The same is true before a regulation becomes a final rule. (The words *rule* and *regulation* are used interchangeably.)

1. **The agency proposes the rule.** Sometimes, the agency creates a draft rule independently; other times, the agency invites interested parties to participate in drafting the proposed rule.
2. **The agency publishes the proposed rule for comment.** Federal rules are published in the *Federal Register*, a daily publication available from the Government Printing Office. Many states also publish public information in registers.
3. **The agency accepts public comment.** During the comment period, the comments can be presented in writing or in person at a public meeting.

4. **Agencies must respond to public comments.** If the response results in major changes to the proposed rule, then the agency must re-propose the rule. However, if changes are minor or if none are made, the agency creates the final rule.
5. **The agency publishes the final rule, generally with some comments.** This occurs after all comment periods are over to let parties know when the rule takes effect and who is subject to the new rule.
6. **The rule is codified in the Code of Federal Regulations or in the state regulatory code.**

Explanation of Regulatory Guidance

Regulatory guidance consists mainly of comments that accompany the rules at various stages of publication. Some agencies also publish separate guidance or policy documents specifically for the purpose of clarifying a confusing rule or explaining the rule's enforcement. Another source of regulatory guidance is agency correspondence to members of the regulated community who formally request regulatory interpretation. These combined sources can go a long way towards explaining a regulation whose meaning is unclear. As mentioned earlier, finding regulatory guidance is relatively simple compared to finding legislative history. Follow the steps in Chapter 6, and you should be on your way.

Rule Tracking

The rule-making process looks at agency thought process and requirements. By contrast, rule tracking focuses on following the actual rule through the rule-making process. Fortunately, doing so is not too difficult, since you generally use the same sources that you used for regulatory guidance. To start, look to the *Federal Register*, or your state version of it, for the publication of proposed rules.

An alternative to searching yourself is to ask the agency to do the work for you. Most agencies maintain lists of interested parties on a variety of issues. If you are interested in an issue, contact the relevant agency and let them know. The agency will then send you notices regarding upcoming rules, the progress of proposed rules, and public meetings regarding those rules.

Research databases are also useful tools in tracking regulations. Both Westlaw (US-REGTRK) and Lexis (FDRGTR) provide specialized directories for tracking regulations. You can also track state regulations by accessing the administrative law section of each individual state. At this time, neither Loislaw nor CD Law offers specialized tools for regulation tracking.

On the Internet, the relevant agency Web page is again your best bet. However, if you are interested in reviewing some opinions along the way, visiting the Web sites of interested parties might also be useful. For example, in 1999 the Federal Deposit Insurance Corporation (FDIC, **www.fdic.gov**) proposed a set of regulations known as the Know Your Customer rules. These rules required banks to monitor its customers larger than normal financial transactions. The regulations aimed to reduce money laundering. Outraged privacy groups posted extensive information about the proposed rules on their Web sites. The groups hoped to get their members to submit comments on the proposed rules during the comment period. The privacy groups achieved astonishing success, causing the agency to withdraw the Know Your Customer rules before they became final. So, visiting Web sites of organizations that might be interested in the outcome of proposed regulation is another good information source during the rulemaking process.

Act *see* statute.

ADJ (adjacent to) Boolean search operator that requires the search terms be adjacent to or next to each other. It is very similar to the phrase operator, but with ADJ, terms can appear in any order.

Administrative agencies a part of the executive branch, administrative agencies have the role of being experts in and advising on a particular area.

ALR (American Law Reports) a secondary source of legal information that has case-specific information.

Bar journal legal periodical aimed at the practicing attorney.

Bill tracking following the process of legislation as it moves from its original proposal through committees to potential passing and signing by the executive.

Bluebook style guide with a uniform system of citation. A small book with a blue cover, Bluebook is used by most legal professionals for proper citation format.

Boolean operator special words used to connect search terms when searching a database.

Browsing looking through ordered lists of information, generally arranged hierarchically, to find information you want. One might browse a table of contents or a subject area of directory.

Case law interpretation of statutory and regulatory law by the judicial branch.

CD-ROM portable disk that can store large quantities of electronic data.

Citation abbreviated method of referring to a source of information. Found in both legal and non-legal documents, citations follow a specific format. In legal writing, the main resource for legal citation format is the Bluebook.

Cite checking *see* Shepardizing.

Code *see* statute.

Codification process of organizing laws according to subject.

Connector *see* Boolean operator.

Database organized collection of information, searchable by keyword.

Default Operator Boolean operator (usually OR) that a database automatically chooses when no Boolean operator is selected.

Defendant party who is being sued at the trial court level.

Dial-up connection using a modem, your computer can call, or dial up, another computer so you can access the information there.

Electronic research looking for answers to questions using computer databases of information.

Et seq Latin phrase meaning *all the following sections*. Statutory citations often use this phrase where the first section of the statute is cited and the rest are included.

Federal Register daily publication issued by the Government Printing Office that includes, among other things, notices on rule making.

Field-restricted search in Westlaw, a search of specific portions of a document like the title, author, parties, etc.

Five Questions a research strategy.

Guidance information an administrative agency gives to help the regulated community comply with regulations.

Hornbook textbook-like, in-depth, and detailed exploration of a broad legal topic like torts or contracts.

Hybrid search tool search tool that contains both a search engine and a search directory.

Internet also known as the Net. A collection of linked computers that lets users review and exchange information. The Internet includes features like e-mail, telnet, bulletin boards, instant messaging, and the World Wide Web.

Internet Service Provider also known as an ISP. The company that gives you access to the Internet, your on-ramp to the information superhighway. ISP facilitates your ability to dial up the Internet through a modem or have constant access to the Internet fast Internet connections.

Issue statement legal question that research aims to answer.

Jurisdiction   as referred to in this chapter, indicates whether a regulation falls under state or federal law.

Keyword   term selected to find relevant documents in a database.

Law review article   article from a legal journal. Law reviews are generally based on detailed research and often focus on specialized topics. They help the researcher to find very in-depth research on detailed topics.

Legal dictionary   resource for word definitions. Specific legal dictionaries are an excellent starting point for research.

Legal encyclopedia   secondary source with brief explanations of legal terms and concepts, often accompanied by references to relevant cases.

Legislative history   documentation of the process that a bill went through to become a law. Often used to interpret the law after its passage.

Meta search tools   search engines that search several search engines at once.

Natural language searching   ability to query a database in the same way that you question a person, without using Boolean operators.

On point   law which specifically addresses some or all of an issue.

Paid legal database   legal database that you can only access by subscribing or paying by the use.

Parallel citation   second location for the same case. For example, a case might be found both in a state reporter and the regional reporter.

Phrase search   searching a database for an exact phrase, with the search terms right next to each other. Quotation marks or parentheses often surround the phrase.

Plaintiff   person who sues at the trial court level.

Practice book   legal reference aimed at the practicing attorney. Often in a three-ring binder, the practice book is meant to be a current reference on everything relevant to its specific subject area.

Proximity search   searching a database for search terms close to each other, usually within 10 to 25 words of each other. This is often indicated with the Boolean operator NEAR.

Query   request to a database for information it contains, using keywords joined by connectors.

Regulated community   businesses and individuals subject to an agency's regulations.

Regulation   also known as a rule. Laws created by administrative agencies to implement statutes. A regulation must have statutory authority granted by the legislature.

Research   looking through information to find the answer to a question.

Research Strategy   plan created to make the researcher think about the research to be done, which thus makes the process more effective. The plan usually includes a determination of relevant law and the best keywords.

Restatement   textbook-like exploration of a single legal subject for which most law is developed in the courts.

Rule   *see* regulation.

Rule-making   process of creating a rule or regulation. The Administrative Procedures Act (APA) sets out the multi-step process at the federal level.

Search directory   search tool that breaks sites into categories to facilitate browsing.

Search engine   tool that lets you search through information on the Internet.

Secondary sources   sources of legal information designed to give you background information and lead you to primary law.

Segment searching   in Lexis, a search of specific portions of a document, such as the title, author, parties, etc.

Shepardizing   generally, the process of checking a law to make sure that it still applies. When Shepardizing cases, you may find other relevant cases that refer to yours. This makes Shepardizing a good research tool.

Specialty search tools   search engines and directories dedicated to specific topics like law or medicine.

Statute   also known as an act or code. A law created by the legislative branch of government.

Stemming   process in which a database automatically looks for common variations of a word, most commonly its plural form.

Stopwords   words that search tools ignore because they appear too frequently. Examples include the words *the*, *of*, and *a*.

Table of Contents   like a book's table of contents, this feature lets you see what sections of the law are available and easily access those sections.

Terms and connectors   used in Lexis to indicate Boolean search operators.

Wildcard operator   symbol used to find variations of a search term. Sometimes called a root expander.

World Wide Web   also known as WWW or the Web. A collection of computers that allows users to access information through an appealing graphical interface. It lets Web sites have images, colors, and other interesting features, rather than just plain text.

(Note: Page numbers in italics refer to figures and tables.)